Nine Pioneers in American Graphic Design

Nine Pioneers in American Graphic Design

R. Roger Remington and Barbara J. Hodik

The MIT Press
Cambridge,
Massachusetts
London,
England

Nine Pioneers in American Graphic Design

This book was set in Univers by Craftsman Type and printed and bound by Dai Nippon Printing Co., Japan.

Library of Congress Cataloging-in-Publication Data

Remington, R. Roger.
Nine pioneers in American graphic design / R. Roger Remington and Barbara J. Hodik.
p. cm.
Bibliography: p.
Includes index.
Contents: An American school — Mehemed Fehmy Agha — Alexey Brodovitch — Charles Coiner — William Golden — Lester Beall — Will Burtin — Alvin Lustig — Ladislav Sutnar — Bradbury Thompson.
ISBN 0-262-18133-9

1. Graphic arts — United States — History — 20th century. 2. Designers — United States — Biography. 3. Commercial art — United States — History — 20th century. I. Hodik, Barbara J. II. Title.
NC998.4.R4 1989
741.6′092′2 — dc19
[B]
88-8980
CIP

To
Beth-Marie Jelsma
and
H. John Jacobi

Contents

Foreword

This book represents an answer to the pressure that has been building up over the last ten years for critical documentation on the work of the pioneers of graphic design in the United States. It addresses the desire to find roots, the desire to have ancestors to whom to refer our ideas, the need to measure our intuitions against a larger history.

We need to see what motivated these pioneers so that we can enrich our theoretical understanding and articulate it in our work. We need to know in order to be. Without history, without theory and criticism, our profession will never come to define itself. Graphic design history can reveal to us not only events but their meanings as well; it can relate the individual artifact to its political, economic, and cultural environment. Design theory can elaborate the ideas and intuitions generated by the issues of the times and relate them to the specifics of design and communication. And, finally, criticism is the instrument that sharpens our tools.

The lives of the designers who shaped our way of seeing and our way of solving problems are lives full of discoveries and personal engagement in their times. Their responses to clients' needs were statements of clear will, uncompromising but appropriate to the task. The moral engagement of Will Burtin, to name one, is an example for us all. We must recognize — and teach those who follow us to recognize — the best works of our profession as the products of an ethical commitment and not merely as a chain of pretty visual feats.

This book advances not only our knowledge of important masters of American graphic design but also our consciousness of the significant place our profession has acquired in contemporary society. Design in general, not only graphic design, is a vital component of the production process, just as essential as economics or manufacturing technology. It is a force that the world has at last come to reckon with.

Roger Remington and Barbara Hodik have been among the primary forces behind the new wave of interest in the history of graphic design. Their Rochester conferences have brought together historians, designers, students, and teachers. For their work in fostering this interest and in advancing the process of documentation, we owe them a debt of gratitude.

Massimo Vignelli

Preface

"The biography of an artist, if his life was sufficiently interesting, is permissible," wrote W. H. Auden, "provided that the biographer and his readers realize that such an account throws no light whatsoever on the artist's work." He added, "I do believe, however, that more often than most people realize, his works may throw light upon his life."[1]

Our research on the nine artists whose stories are told in this book has convinced us that for each of them, "the meaning of life lies," in Rollo May's words, "in creating, leaving something for future generations."[2] Our purpose here is to help those future generations to understand and remember what it is that these graphic design pioneers created, what is the nature of their legacy.

Over the past thirty combined years of teaching, we both have observed blank looks on the faces of students when the names or works of their ancestors in graphic design were mentioned in the course of our lecture or studio classes. As we thought about reasons for our students' lack of historical knowledge, we realized that in spite of the rapid growth of graphic design as a shaper of cultural values and attitudes in the twentieth century, art historians typically concentrate on the fine arts of painting, drawing, sculpture, and architecture. The history of the applied arts is rarely dealt with and even more rarely taught in art history graduate programs. As a result, little scholarly attention has been paid to documenting graphic design and designers. The letters, sketches, mechanicals, and produced work of designers have not generally been considered worthy of archival treatment; much primary and secondary source material has thus been lost to researchers and scholars. Over the past several years our own experience in seeking out printed reference material and resources on pioneers in graphic design history has been frustrating, to say the least.

Graphic design is an emerging profession; it exists largely in the minds of those engaged in that work. It is also, as Robert Jensen puts it, a "mongrel profession,"[3] combining the separate disciplines of photography, printing and typography, art, and advertising. These have begun to converge into one discipline known as graphic design only in the last sixty years; and yet graphic design, through its sheer pervasiveness in our society, affects more people than do the best of the traditional fine arts. The producers of high-impact design often remain anonymous, however—except to other practicing designers who might be working in the same geographic area or in the same branch of the profession.

In an attempt to determine for ourselves the "state of the art" of graphic design history, we originated, developed, and conducted two international symposia, which each drew over two hundred noted graphic designers, teachers of graphic design, and students to the Rochester Institute of Technology in 1983 and 1985. The participants agreed unanimously that bodies of graphic design history in book form are sorely needed. The designer and educator Louis Danziger stressed that before the writers of graphic design history can begin to aim for depth, accurate material on the level of people, events, work, and chronology is needed. Symposia attendees concluded that because there is a difference between what practicing designers can do in graphic design history and what art historians can do, attempts should be made to write graphic design history cooperatively. This book is the product of such a cooperation.

Following extensive consultations with historians, teachers, practitioners, and friends of the profession, a list of pioneering designers emerged. The criteria for selection were these: the designer should have done his major work·in the United States, and during the period between the late 1920s and the early 1970s; through his work, the designer should have helped shape graphic design as a profession and have made a distinctive and innovative contribution; the designer's story has not been told recently or, if it has, it is fragmented in periodicals and needs to be presented as a whole; the designer's mature work was accomplished in New York or its environs — this last because of the historic importance of the City to the profession, the context it provided for a kind of synergistic development.

It was difficult to narrow our list to the nine eventually included — M. F. Agha, Alexey Brodovitch, Charles Coiner, William Golden, Lester Beall, Will Burtin, Alvin Lustig, Ladislav Sutnar, and Bradbury Thompson. Paul Rand, for example, belongs in this group of pioneers. By himself he is a giant and responsible for a great deal of the history of graphic design. We felt, however, that a considerable amount of current information about him was available through his own books and in periodicals. Others, such as Egbert Jacobson, have also made major contributions, but in a specialized or regional context. Many who worked in the allied fields of advertising and promotion — Helmut Krone, Jack Tinker, and Bob Gage, for example — need mentioning. Because of the limits set on career opportunities for women during the formative period within which the selected designers worked, no women are included. When the story of the next generation of graphic designers is told, women will have their rightful places among the best contributors.

Once our list of subjects was determined, we interviewed the two still living—Charles Coiner and Bradbury Thompson—and the families, colleagues, and friends of the dead. We surveyed the existing literature, analyzed the work of the designers, and gathered representative examples of that work in order to provide visual documentation. Each designer is considered in the framework of his education, his use of milieu, his methods of visual problem solving and client relations, his work, and his philosophy of design.

Like pioneers in other fields, the nine men in this book have provided maps of hitherto uncharted territory that allow future generations to understand the terrain. Their maps are quite different from one another, although there is a common quality: all these graphic designers were visual problem solvers primarily concerned with creating functional visual communication. László Moholy-Nagy (1895–1946), the Bauhaus designer, called the artist/designer a "refined seismograph of his time because he has an intuitive ability to record matters pertaining to the future in a language based upon sensory experience"; employing, as we have done, the image of the mapmaker, he characterized the visual artist as one who could "give symbolic representation of the terrain—or the upheavals—characteristic of any one society."[4] We hope that this book will contribute to a better understanding of the process by which these pioneers created their works of symbolic representation, and to a better understanding of the historical significance of those works.

Acknowledgments

We wish to thank the following individuals and organizations, without whose support, information, and encouragement this book would not have been possible:

Walter Allner

Sr. Alma Mary Anderson, C.S.C.

Sam Antiput

Richard Avedon

Dorothy Beall (deceased)

Linda Blake

Karen M. Bloom

Joseph V. Bower

Aaron Burns

Laurie Burns

Sharon Candell

Bob Cato

Robert Coates

Arthur A. Cohen (deceased)

Elaine Lustig Cohen

Charles Coiner

Roger Conover

Mildred Constantine

Louise Dahl-Wolfe

Louis Danziger

Carolyn Davis

Claire DeFillippo

Lou Dorfsman

Debbi Edelstein

Carol Burtin Fripp

Shelley Frydman

Howard Gardner

Nathan Gluck

Tom Golden

Betti Broadwater Haft

Michele Italiano

Diane Jaroch

Beth-Marie Jelsma

Robert H. Johnston

Burton Kramer

George Lois

Juan Lopez-Bonilla

Jessica Loy

Brad Lynch

Kimberly Mackowiak

John Malinoski

Sandra Maniscalco

Sandra Markham

Philip B. Meggs

Holly Mitchell

Joyce Morrow

Paul Neville

Arnold Newman

Cipe Pineles

Peter Plante

Barbara Polowy

Elton S. Robinson

Allon T. Schoener

Tina Selak

Michael Soluri

Claudia Stata

Radoslav Sutnar

Gladys Taylor

Bradbury Thompson

Massimo Vignelli

Carol Wahler

Lynda Wanzenreid

Shelly Webster

Kurt Weihs

Joanna Beall Westermann

Henry Wolf

Frank Zachary

American Institute of Graphics Arts

George Arents Research Library, Syracuse University

N. W. Ayer and Company

Museum of Modern Art

Rochester Institute of Technology, College of Fine and Applied Arts, Graphic Design Archive

Rochester Institute of Technology Archives

Sweet's Division, McGraw-Hill Information Systems Company

Type Directors Club of New York

Westvaco Corporation

Nine Pioneers in American Graphic Design

Nine Pioneers in American Graphic Design

An American School

American society between the two world wars experienced particularly strong upheavals; for aspiring artists and designers, it offered great opportunities for rebuilding and breaking new ground. The specious economic boom of the 1920s — which promised, in F. Scott Fitzgerald's phrase, everything that could be expected "this side of paradise" — was answered inevitably by the depression of the 1930s. Many Americans left their rural or small-town homes for the cities, in search of better opportunities, or at least survival. Economic and social turmoil in Europe during the 1930s led a number of artists to emigrate to the United States, and with them came the ideas of the European avant-garde.

From California the young Charles Coiner moved east, first to Chicago and then to Philadelphia, where he became an innovative art director at N. W. Ayer, developing there an outstanding creative organization that would change the look of American advertising. At twenty-seven, Bradbury Thompson left Topeka, Kansas, for New York, where he would spend many years extending the boundaries of corporate, magazine, and book design. Lester Beall, born in Kansas City, Missouri, established his first office in Chicago, but he too eventually settled in New York. He was among the first to open an office of graphic design. His work would transform the appearance of American corporations and products. William Golden, born in New York, returned after some years in California. Golden would elevate the standards of promotion at CBS Television and prove that the graphic designer belongs in a position of responsibility. Alvin Lustig, who grew up in California, brought a new look to hundreds of book jackets in New York in the 1940s and 1950s. Just as important as his contributions to the book publishing business were his innovations in a variety of other areas, from signage to interior design.

From Berlin and Paris in the late 1920s came M. F. Agha and Alexey Brodovitch. Through his design and art direction of *Vanity Fair* and other Condé Nast magazines, Agha would elevate America's standards of magazine design, printing, and photography. Brodovitch, too, would become an innovator in magazine design, spending most of his career at *Harper's Bazaar.* He would share new ideas with many young photographers, thus profoundly influencing photography as we know it today. In the late 1930s, with World War II on the horizon, Will Burtin emigrated from Germany. His work for scientific and technical clients would translate complex information into understandable messages for industrial, commercial, and educational purposes. Ladislav Sutnar of Czechoslovakia, stranded in New York at the outbreak of World War II, stayed on. His unique skills at organization would benefit many industrial and commercial clients.

These young designers persevered through the hard times of the 1930s and the chaos of World War II. The latter saw many of them designing for the United States government in various capacities. During the war, very few goods were available for consumer purchase. Advertising had nothing to sell. When the war ended, the scene changed dramatically to a buyer's market. Designers finally had the opportunity to express their ideas in the spheres of advertising and communication. Aaron Burns, president of the International Typeface Corporation, recalls:

Everything began after World War II. During the war a number of these pioneers were brought together at the Office of War Information. After the war they became the leaders. It was all new and exciting work. This was a new scene for designers in dealing with typography too. They were able to see the problem of what needed to be communicated, select the elements, assign proper weights and sizes of type in an arrangement that would be interesting. Asymmetry was the style then (as it also was in architecture) and the order of the day.[1]

Lou Dorfsman, who worked under William Golden at CBS in the 1940s and 1950s, has similar memories:

Before this time, a Yale man would bring something in [to the art department] and ask that you "make it nice." This was the style in the thirties and forties. Only the Yale men were the thinkers. The big lesson here was that the creative people were learning to have arrogance or chutzpah and that they indeed could think!

He cites another important change as well:

In 1949, the advertising/communications business, which had been very white, Anglo-Saxon, Protestant, broke wide open. You suddenly had Jews, Greeks, all kinds of people in the business, who gave it an incredible shot in the arm. All kinds of wonderful, crazy things happened. The changes were due to this ethnic influx in addition to the fat, rich U.S.A.[2]

Lorraine Wild has noted the influence of the Europeans on the changing role of the graphic designer. The European preference for "modern" images that were created mechanically over hand-drawn forms was consistent with the age of the machine, and the mechanization of image production helped to emphasize the role of the designer as thinker, "selecting, editing, creating in the mind, rather than producing with the hand."[3]

Survivors of a depression and a world war, inheritors of the modernist machine ethic, and promulgators of the role of designer as thinker, the nine designers discussed in this book can be called an "American School." Not only did they hold certain views in common, but they also often met and talked with one another—at the Art Directors Club, the Type Directors Club, the American Institute of Graphics Arts, the gallery at Robert Leslie's Composing Room, the A-D Gallery, the Museum of Modern Art. MOMA, owing to the pioneering efforts of its associate curator, Mildred Constantine, was sponsoring exhibits and programs on graphic design. Constantine recalls that "there was a common spirit in this period.

M. F. Agha and an unidentified juror discussing work submitted for the 1952 AIGA "Printing for Commerce" exhibit. Courtesy AIGA Archives.

The 1949 AIGA "Printing for Commerce" exhibit judges included Ladislav Sutnar *(left)*, Will Burtin *(center)*, and William Golden *(right)* Courtesy AIGA Archives

The jury for the AIGA "Design and Printing for Commerce" exhibit, 1954. *Left to right:* William Golden, M.F. Agha, Joseph Blumenthal, Ariosto Nardozzi, Alvin Lustig. Joyce Morrow Collection, Rochester Institute of Technology.

These pioneers had a sense of history and the importance of the new ground they were breaking. At MOMA we recognized this too. For me, graphics reflected the best of all the arts."[4]

There were innovative meetings such as the forum "TDC '26–'36, Inspired Typography," produced by Aaron Burns and sponsored by the Type Directors Club of New York. The goal of this historic series of educational programs was to make visible a "clear, revealing, stimulating picture of how today's design developed, where it is leading and why," according to the invitation for the series. The invitation credits Lester Beall, Alexey Brodovitch, Ladislav Sutnar, and others, such as Herbert Bayer, A. M. Cassandre, and Jan Tschichold, as among the designers who "led the way." Burns identifies a second group who advanced the ideas of the first, namely, Will Burtin, William Golden, Alvin Lustig, Bradbury Thompson, and others such as Saul Bass, Leo Lionni, Herbert Lubalin, and Paul Rand. In the late 1950s Burns also organized the seminal "Typography-U.S.A." forum on the theme "What Is New in American Typography?" with Will Burtin as program chairman. Of the nine subjects of this volume, Beall, Burtin, Golden, Sutnar, and Thompson were presentors at this meeting, along with thirteen other designers. Lou Dorfsman remembers the period as being "made up of an amalgam of wonderful people. They showed the way to a new path – straightforward, extraordinary, honest, and provocative."[5]

There were close friendships among these nine pioneers, and professional relationships as well. Golden worked for Agha at Condé Nast Publications during the thirties. Over the years several designers worked for the same clients and on the same projects. Lester Beall and later Will Burtin worked on *Scope* magazine for the Upjohn Company. *Scope*, sent by the pharmaceutical company to physicians, became a prime example of how to translate complex subject matter into understandable and beautiful images. Brodovitch, Lustig, and Sutnar designed covers for *Fortune* magazine, and Will Burtin was art director at *Fortune* from 1945 to 1949. Robert Leslie of the Composing Room featured articles, inserts, or complete issues of his publications *PM* (Production Manager) and *A-D* (Art Director) on Agha, Beall, Brodovitch, Burtin, and Coiner; and the A-D Gallery, sponsored by the Composing Room, held exhibits of the work of most of the nine.

Five of these designers – Brodovitch, Burtin, Coiner, Lustig, and Thompson – devoted a significant part of their time to teaching, whether in the university classroom or in small, informal seminars or workshops. Most also regularly participated in national conferences. Will Burtin was particularly active as an organizer of and speaker at educational meetings.

The majority of the pioneers in our group not only were versatile designers but also worked in some branch of the fine arts. Coiner had a major one-man exhibition of his paintings at the Midtown Gallery in New York in 1986. Beall designed an experimental audio component, the stereophonic music sphere for ALCOA; Brodovitch designed and fabricated low-cost furniture with rope and plywood; Burtin designed an architectural structure for the New York World's Fair; Lustig designed a one-man helicopter. Sutnar wrote extensively about the basis for his design and was widely published. Thompson has designed a number of United States commemorative stamps.

Together, they expanded the limited fields of commercial art and printing in the 1940s and 1950s to include a new visual vocabulary that embraced both art and technology and gave shape to the new profession of graphic design. They understood the necessity of a marriage of form and content. Most were self-taught and developed their own versions of modernism by being acutely sensitive to the changes in the visual world around them. Whether through the creation of corporate identity programs, through magazine, book, or poster design, through exhibit design, advertising, or signage, these nine leading members of the American school of graphic design have, in Faulkner's words, "created out of the materials of the human spirit something which did not exist before."[6] We have much to learn from their work.

Mehemed Fehmy Agha   1896–1978

The middle son of three, Mehemed Fehmy Agha was born on March 3, 1896, to Turkish parents in Nikolayev, a Ukrainian shipping port on the Black Sea.[1] Agha's father, the descendant of an ancient family of Turkish Cypriot merchants, had delayed marriage until he was well into his fifties because he was searching for a woman with the proper bloodlines. Following the family tradition, he was a tobacco dealer and importer of olives, oil in leather skins, and spices brought into Russia by camel caravan across Turkey. Mehemed and his brothers, Abram and Jacques, grew up in a walled family compound that included storage and sales areas patrolled by a live-in night watchman.

From childhood, Agha's gifts were evident; he had published a book of drawings by the time he was seventeen. As a young man he sold illustrations and cartoons to magazines, though his only formal art education consisted of a brief period of study at the Academy of Fine Arts in Kiev, which he left to pursue an interest in political science. He also studied economics at the Emperor Peter the Great Polytechnic Institute.

When World War I was beginning, Agha's father sent his sons out of the country. In order that they might establish themselves once safely abroad, he provided them with fine clothing with gold coins sewn into the hems. Soldiers robbed them, however, before they had got outside Russia. Although M. F. Agha was to search for many years, he never learned the fate of his father or of the family holdings. Later in life, Agha claimed that before his departure he had served on the staff of Kerensky, a moderate socialist who would briefly head the revolutionary government of Russia before being himself overthrown by the Bolsheviks in November 1917. One of his classmates in school, Agha said, had been Andrei Gromyko, who would become an eminent Soviet diplomat. Indeed, he hinted, had he not left Russia in accordance with his father's wishes, he would have been involved in the highest levels of Russian politics.[2]

Agha next spent a few years in Paris, where in 1923 he received a diploma from the National School of Modern Oriental Languages. Stories abound about how he learned the many languages he spoke. Because he was such a showman and leg-puller, one cannot be certain of the truth of any of them — only that he could speak Russian, German, French, Turkish, and English. Agha claimed, for example, to have learned to read English by the age of five, by examining the English newspapers lining the clothes chest of a Scottish nanny his parents had engaged. Another story, however, had him learning English from an Irish teacher in Berlin.

It was while working for German *Vogue* in Berlin in 1928 that Agha encountered Condé Nast, the man who brought him to the United States to be art director of Condé Nast Publications. That year, Heyworth Campbell had resigned as art director of American *Vogue*. It had become apparent that the magazine needed a new look. A new visual age had been heralded by the 1925 Paris Exposition of Modern Decorative and Industrial Arts and by the architecture of Le Corbusier; but under Campbell's staid direction, *Vogue* had languished in old-school decoration, classical type, and dense layout. Nast, together with Frank Crowninshield, the editor of *Vanity Fair*, and Edna Woolman Chase, the editor of *Vogue*, traveled to London, Paris, and Berlin (Nast was publishing foreign editions in these European capitals) to find a replacement for Campbell. They found German *Vogue* in dire financial straits due to runaway inflation and the resultant diminishment of interest in fashion. The lack of consumers meant lack of advertising, and the temporary disappearance of an upwardly mobile middle class meant no readership for *Vogue*. Shortly after Christmas Nast closed German *Vogue*, but not before hiring its greatest asset, the monacled art director M. F. Agha. Concerning the impact Agha made on him, Nast wrote:

After I had passed a few days in Berlin, I began seeing more and more of [Agha's] work. There were so many evidences in it of order, taste, and invention that I began thinking of him as a possible Art Director for our American periodicals. Before leaving Berlin I spent a morning with him in discussing type, engraving, illustration, and layout. It was at that conference that my opinions underwent a singular psychological change with regard to Turks in general, and Russian Turks in particular.[3]

Nast and Agha could not have been more different in background, tastes, and temperament; yet the two worked well together—the self-effacing publisher counterbalanced the flamboyant, acerbic, cynical art director.

The Years at Condé Nast

Dr. Agha, as he liked to be called—the "doctor" dating from his days in Berlin, where according to German custom anyone of a scholarly persuasion might be so addressed—engineered the visual development of Condé Nast's magazines between 1929 and 1943. Immediately on his arrival he began to put in place the policies that would change the look of *Vogue*, *Vanity Fair*, and *House and Garden*. Agha's was a presence that made itself felt: his colleague Frank Crowninshield recalled, ten years after Agha's advent, how he "first occupied a single room in the *Vogue* offices but was very shortly occupying two, then four and then six. He spread out so fast that an additional floor had to be engaged at the Graybar Building in order to prevent him bulging out the windows, going through the roof or occupying the elevator shafts and ladies room."[4]

Agha believed that American advertising had tolerated routine, mundane appearances for years. His keen understanding of the European avant-garde artists and designers led him to believe that Constructivism was basic to almost everything that was described as "modern" in the 1930s: "The temple of Constructivism," he wrote, "is full of treasures and is therefore recommended to the commercial designer for new inspirations."[5] In addition to providing overall direction, Agha took photographs, wrote articles, rebuilt the photography studio, and helped with cover designs, type fonts, captions, dress patterns, engraving, and color printing. Of the role of the art director, he once said:

His field is usually limited to commercial, advertising, graphic and other non-fine arts. In this field he is the autocrat of the drawing table, with authority restricted only by the requirements of team work, research findings, editorial policies, client's preferences, reader's mental age and publisher's niece. . . . He is the first cousin of the movie director, and like the movie director, he plans, coordinates and rehearses, but does not perform; at least not in public.[6]

The art director must lead popular taste, not follow it, Agha maintained:

His barometer is . . . a very finely adjusted instrument. It disregards small accidental atmospheric changes, little showers of bad taste, puny tornadoes of hard boiled ugliness. It records only the sounder and broader tendencies and trends.[7]

Joyce Morrow, former director of the American Institute of Graphic Arts, describes Agha's mind as a "perfect sponge and sieve." He possessed a prodigious ability to absorb knowledge. Voracious for new information, technical details, or intellectual challenges, he would quickly become bored and would need to move on to something else. Another co-worker referred to him as "the man who knew too much to like anything." There was an unsettled quality about him. Some thought—and sardonic remarks by Agha himself bore them out—that his restlessness and air of dissatisfaction arose from a distaste for publishing design. "Personally," he once said, "I might be inclined to [the view] that a fashion magazine's conception of beauty, elegance and taste might be insipid and nauseating, but I firmly believe that a fashion magazine is not the place to display our dislikes for these things."[8] Those who knew Agha best characterized him as not really belonging in the world of magazine publication. According to Cipe Pineles, a member of the art department at *Vogue* in the thirties, "Agha never liked graphic design to begin with; he simply fell into it. He was a major figure who should have had a career in the political or diplomatic arena."[9] In an essay for the 1939 *PM* magazine issue devoted to Agha, William Golden, who had also worked for him before

Two-page spread from "Agha's American Decade," *PM* magazine issue of 1939. A note to Robert Leslie from Francis Brennan, art director of *Fortune* magazine, is juxtaposed with a drawing of Agha. In the note Brennan suggests what it was like to work for Agha. Black and white; 11" × 7⅞".

Two-page spread from *PM* issue on Agha. Here Agha's character is read from his handprint. Black and red.

Caricature of Agha by Dugo, from *PM* issue "Agha's American Decade."

joining the CBS staff, observed: "Mehemed Fehmy Agha is an unhappy man. He has learned nearly all there is to know about the graphic arts, only to discover that he never liked them in the first place." Agha, Golden continued,

had spent a great deal of time with the graphic arts, and gained some recognition for his brilliance, only to discover that the whole thing was pretty dull in itself. He didn't like the stuff that people called Art . . . and which he called making pictures. The people that made the pictures had an uncanny knack for making them, but on the whole, they were a pretty limited lot and possibly part idiot.[10]

This questioning, analytic approach — a refusal to accept anything as sacred — extended to all branches of the arts. Frank Crowninshield commented that Agha's "approach to art was almost like that of an anthropologist — he was curious as to how things were done, by what kind of people, reacting under what kind of pressure, but remained himself entirely the objective observer."[11] And in an article about the photographer Ralph Steiner, Agha spoke of Steiner in words that could apply equally well to himself: "he can be compared to a whale whose sole effort is to open its mouth while swimming about and swallow the small fish which happen to come his way."[12] His mind's capacity to absorb ideas and concepts and then to juxtapose them in unusual ways fostered the habit of intellectual stretching, so it was natural for him to expect the same from his staff members. Joyce Morrow remembers William Golden's comments about what it was like to work for Agha at Condé Nast:

Agha would present you with a problem, a little page. "Bring me something with three variations." He would then look at the work and he would say, "Well, this is satisfactory, but I am sure that it is possible for you to do more." We'd go out and do thirteen other solutions, straining ourselves, scraping the bottom of the barrel. Agha would look at these and he'd say, "Well, that's much better, but I feel we need more." We'd come back with another ten and he'd say "Well, the second one you brought me was the best in the lot."[13]

When asked if he felt that Agha's approach was cruel, Golden replied, "No, it stretched us out. It was not cruel at all. You could never please him; in fact, he could never please himself."[14] Golden would learn criticism well from Agha. During his career at CBS Television, Golden expected his staff to push themselves beyond what they felt capable of doing: "I submit that an artist who's suspicious of his own work is most likely to look for new forms of expression."[15]

One of Agha's staff artists remembered that Agha's "role was to keep the mold of self-satisfaction from forming and to make co-workers ever suspect of things shoddy. If his criticism stunned, it was to stir the artists and designers about him to search deeper within themselves for the answers they could not foresee to graphic problems."[16] Agha's demands were simple: make work legible, logical, and luxurious in a way that would appeal to *him.* Another co-worker said, "He liked

absolutely nothing. I was a fairly important editor and it pleased him to make me cry tears of rage . . . and then we went to lunch."[17]

Agha never taught formal classes. Yet for some of his colleagues he was an important teacher. Condé Nast said that he could never pretend to give instruction around Agha, because Agha had "assumed that role himself—after relegating me politely to the dunce's corner where, apparently, he thought I really belonged."[18] Golden called Agha "a professor who gave you a great deal, with whom you study intensely for a year, eight hours a day."[19] Cipe Pineles recalls:

I had a special privilege because by the time I was hired, there was no room in the bullpen, so my desk was wedged in behind some file cabinets in Agha's office. I was in on all the talk. He spent a lot of time talking with his creative people, going over ideas for them to develop. We talked about problems that related to type, pictures and selection of pictures as satisfying an editorial concept or not. Agha gave us lots of rope to hang ourselves. So we didn't do just one solution to a problem. I would try a solution two or three times. All those trials were the luxury part of the job.[20]

Pineles also feels that Agha had a particular sensitivity to the problems facing women in the profession. It was he who persuaded her to apply to the New York Art Directors Club for admission as the first woman member. She did so, but it took the club nearly five years to grant her entrance. A counterpoint to Pineles's observations, however, is provided by a *Vogue* editor who worked with Agha—a woman, as were nearly all the editors and copywriters:

His point of view was that no woman was as important as a man. Compared to a man who was a fool, a foolish woman was more so. He wouldn't fight for an editorial point with a man and show the same annoyance with which he'd fight a woman.[21]

Free-lance artists were encouraged to consider features in which they might be interested. Agha maintained a free, creative atmosphere in the department.

Full-color illustration by Cipe Pineles, a member of the art department at *Vogue* in the 1930s. The depiction of Agha as surrounded by women staffers, many in hats and fashionable attire, is faithful to the "way it was then," according to Pineles. This illustration was included in "Agha's American Decade," an issue of *PM* magazine documenting Agha's work between 1930 and 1939. *PM* was produced by The Composing Room, Inc., under the visionary leadership of Robert Leslie. 5⅜" × 7¾".

He encouraged the staff to use working time to visit exhibits and museums for inspiration and research.

Agha's strong technical background enabled him to relate easily with photographers and printers. He set up and conducted complicated engineering experiments in an effort to give the artist and photographer a printed page in color that was worthy of the art that graced it. He created a fully equipped photographic studio in his office in order to conduct tests and research. He shared the results with others, particularly the photographers whom he hired for magazine assignments. Pineles remembers Agha and Edward Steichen having many talks about lighting. When Cecil Beaton came to work at *Vogue* in the winter of 1928, he used a snapshot camera and had his old nanny develop his film at home in the bathtub. Though Nast had urged him to get a better camera, it took a letter from Agha in 1929 to get Beaton to upgrade his camera technology. Agha wrote to Beaton that *Vogue* was having problems developing his photos:

I think that all the defaults are due to the fact that you are using a small camera, and submit your photographs to too great enlargements that make the grey surfaces to lose consistency, and sometimes make the figures look muddy. . . . Mr. Nast likes your photographs very much for their qualities of charm and good composition and is very anxious to see you improve their technical qualities.[22]

Agha was an innovator in practical art studio tools and processes, such as preprinted layout grid sheets for the designers to use in creating double-page spreads. He had sheets of preprinted dummy type, including Bodoni Book, so his designers could cut and paste for type indication. Copy was always shown with this dummy type. He had a photostat machine installed in the art department and encouraged the staff to make dummy layouts as finished as possible for presentation, a process used later by Golden and his CBS staff. Agha introduced bleed photographs, about which he wrote in *American Printer*:

In December, 1930, we had the bright idea of printing a picture bleed-edged, the first picture, to our knowledge, to be so printed in any magazine on this continent. There was good reason for the bleed in this because it was a picture of a parachute in the sky. A sky is a very big thing, so the bigger you make it, the better off you are — which raises the question of what pictures are suitable for bleed edges. When I was a child I had a book of animals, and the small animals all had nice frames around them. The larger animals were bigger, but the elephant was so big he was bleed-edged. His forehead was on one side of the book and his tail on the other. That is legitimate bleed-edging, taking something big and showing it big.[23]

Condé Nast Publications owned the engraving and printing plants that produced the magazines, so it was possible for Agha to work closely with technical experts. He was especially concerned with upgrading the quality of printing. Pineles recalls that Agha pioneered the use of duotone effects in printing: "I remember him reproducing black and white in duotone using two colors that looked like one. This was very innovative. I also remember him specifying the number of times he wanted the duotone proofed, so he could explore what happened when browns got warmer and warmer as they combined with black. Duotones were featured as something pretty special."[24]

Agha moved the Condé Nast magazines away from a restrictive, antiquarian approach to page design, illustration, and photography by applying his experience with European avant-garde art and design to *Vogue*, *Vanity Fair*, and *House and Garden*. One aspect of the dramatic change was the use of sans serif types (Intertype Vogue) set by machine. It was not long before over 40 percent of the advertising pages also used sans serif faces. He banished the use of italic types, changed the shape of the headlines, and made greater use of white space. Nast provided support for these dramatic changes because he was aware that the success of the magazines depended to a large degree upon a commitment to be modern.

Agha's interest in photography led to another remarkable change: a new treatment of subjects that emphasized their being expressive and alive. He would crop photographs tightly and use silhouette effects. In addition, he brought into the fold the most brilliant photographers of the day, including Edward Steichen, George Hoyningen-Huené, Horst, Louise Dahl-Wolfe, Edward Weston, Berenice Abbott, and Toni Frissell.

The year 1932 was a banner year for graphic innovations in *Vogue*: the first full-color photograph appeared in April, the first color cover by Steichen in July, and the first bleed page in September. The new format was provocative and controversial. When Edna Woolman Chase, *Vogue*'s editor, confronted Agha with readers' negative responses, he replied, "It is a good thing to try to show everybody that we are still alive and leaders in the field of typographic mode. We have been the first on the market to produce this kind of Germanic type for machine setting, and all the others are following us."[25] He was able to show with precise statistics how advertisers were changing over to sans serif types. This mass of supportive data pleased Nast and silenced Chase.

The relationship between a magazine's own style and the styles of its advertisements was of course a matter of concern for Agha. Though he was responsible for the innovations in design and layout in *Vogue* and *Vanity Fair*, he wryly assigned much of the credit for such innovations to advertising. In an article

Cover for *Vanity Fair*, July 1933, with illustration by Paolo Garretto. Under Agha's art direction, important artists and caricaturists were regularly used to make political comment on the covers. The dimensions of *Vanity Fair* throughout the 1930s were 9¾" × 12¾".

Page from the July 1934 issue of *Vanity Fair*, with photograph by Edward Steichen. This image, which became an icon of the era, was created by overprinting several photographs of New York skyscrapers.

Two-page spread from *Vanity Fair*, February 1934, with the heads of President Roosevelt and other government figures superimposed on a football team to show their political persuasions.

Two-page spread from *Vanity Fair*, August 1934. This complex illustration, which pokes fun at celebrities of the day, shows the use of bleed edges and color reproduction, both unusual for the time.

Cover for *Vanity Fair*, July 1934, with color photograph by Anton Bruehl. Agha pushed graphic arts technology to new frontiers. This early full-color printed cover, which bleeds on four sides, features Clifton Webb, Jimmy Savo, and Irene Dunne. The complicated process of photographing the cover was described on the title page of the issue at some length. The description concluded with this comment: "You do not see all this—and you probably do not care. But this will give you just a rough idea of what we go through for our public. Anyway, we had a lot of fun."

written in 1968, he indicated that it was advertising which shaped the size, layout, and techniques of magazines. Indeed, he continued,

This was not enough for advertising. In the constant competition for public attention that has so many demands on it in our age, advertising, during the last thirty years or so, has developed eye-catching, tradition-breaking techniques, mostly borrowed from the post-world-war-one-modern art: bleed pages, giant gatefolds, abstract symbolism, off-beat plots, syncopated piggy-back typography, giant faces, Victorian revivals, giant body-type, and various other creative ding bats. The glorious sport of eye-catching was fashionably called *visual communication*.[26]

If *Vogue* was the fashion leader of this period, then *Vanity Fair* was the arts and culture showcase of America. Crowninshield declared its editorial creed: to believe in the progress and promise of American life and to chronicle that progress cheerfully, truthfully, and entertainingly. Under his enlightened leadership *Vanity Fair* developed three distinguishing strengths: an elegant and stylish layout, connection with the artistic avant-garde community, and literary pieces of high quality. In *Vanity Fair* Agha was showing works by Matisse, Maillol, Derain, Pascin, Kolbe, Laurencin, Mestrovic, Kent, Covarrubias, and Picasso years before any other American magazine did. The use of illustrations by noted artists was a major contribution of Agha's, to be continued later by Golden at CBS Television, Pineles at *Seventeen*, Brodovitch at *Harper's Bazaar*, and Coiner at N. W. Ayer.

A delight to the eyes of both the expert and the ordinary reader, *Vanity Fair* provided Agha an open field for visual experimentation. He extended letterspacing in type, ran the type flush with the page margins, used heavy black bars and dingbat symbols, and put away any "decorative" elements. He even introduced headlines and captions without any capital letters, as seen in designs by Herbert Bayer. However, when Agha produced an entire issue in lowercase type, readers were so incensed that he never dared try it again.

Agha preserved the three-column format and preferred to design the magazine as sequences of double-page spreads, rather than separate pages. This method, later used by Ladislav Sutnar and Alexey Brodovitch, gave the magazine a unity and a more powerful visual presence. The May 1930 issue of *Vanity Fair* introduced the double-page spread, using a Steichen photograph. Pineles recalls that Agha, "in an attempt to do everything *he* could, allowed *us* to do everything, including turning pages around, so that sometimes I would do a double-page spread the long way. Mr. Nast called a meeting at one point in which he requested that we do layouts so that the title would be 'in the expected place.'"[27]

VANITY FAIR

JULY 1934 © THE CONDÉ NAST PUBLICATIONS, INC. PRICE 35 CENTS

This cover for *Vanity Fair*, June 1934, by Paolo Garretto, was titled, "The brain trust and the capitol." The academic cap and gown juxtaposed atop the U.S. Capitol building created an iconic unity of meaning.

Cover for *Vanity Fair*, September 1934, with illustration by Paolo Garretto. The National Recovery Administration's Blue Eagle (designed by Charles Coiner) has got hold of an apprehensive Uncle Sam. A controversial program, the NRA was voted out by Congress in May 1935.

Cover for *Vanity Fair*, August 1934, by the French painter Raoul Dufy.

Cover for *Vanity Fair*, November 1934. The Mexican caricaturist and illustrator Miguel Covarrubias shows the Blue Eagle being offered up by President Roosevelt.

Cover for *Vanity Fair*, January 1935, designed to fold up in such a way as to show either a very thin Uncle Sam or a fat one.

Cover for *Vanity Fair*, December 1934, with a witty Christmas message on the state of world armaments by Paolo Garretto. The pages of *Vanity Fair* were predicting the coming of World War II five years before its start.

Cover for *Vanity Fair*, February 1935, with illustration by Paolo Garretto. A hot international topic, the rise of imperial Japan, is treated in this powerful visual statement.

Cover for *Vanity Fair*, March 1935, by Paolo Garretto. This illustration captures the manipulative nature of Roosevelt as the puppeteer, pulling the strings for the battle between the rich and the workers.

Page from *Vanity Fair* from the
1930s, advertising its *Portfolio of
Modern French Art*. Through the
magazine, Agha and others regularly contributed to America's
cultural broadening by displaying
the best works of European artists and making reproductions
available to the public. This
ad features a diagram by Miguel
Covarrubias, entitled "The Tree
of Modern Art—Showing the
Correlation of the Various
Schools and Movements."

Two-page spread from *Vanity
Fair*, September 1934, with black
and white photographic portraits
of Gary Cooper and Katharine
Hepburn by George Hoyningen-
Huené. Agha employed the finest
photographers of the period.
Himself an expert on photographic technique, he worked
closely with his photographers.

Two-page spread from *Vanity
Fair*, October 1935. Color snap-
shots by Edward Steichen catch
members of the Radio City
Music Hall ballet midair as they
execute a series of leaps.

Page from *Vanity Fair*, February 1936, with a regular feature, "Impossible Interview" —an imaginary conversation between incongruous figures. This illustration by Miguel Covarrubias shows classical musician Fritz Kreisler with jazz trumpeter Louis Armstrong. Color.

Two page spread from the February 1936 *Vanity Fair*, with black-and-white photographs by Edward Steichen. The subject was the dance team of Grace and Paul Hartman. This presentation shows the way dance can be communicated through layout, overlapping, bleed photographs, and size progression.

After Nast

Agha's best years were at Condé Nast Publications. After Nast's death in 1942, Agha's position as art director was less than secure; and in 1943 he was replaced by Alexander Liberman. Following his departure from Condé Nast Publications, he worked as a designer and consultant for insurance companies, department stores, and publishing companies that specialized in advertising and promotional work. He was also a consultant for the Leo Burnett Advertising Agency in Chicago, providing a monthly critique of the work of the creative departments. Active in the American Institute of Graphic Arts, he served for several years as its president. Joyce Morrow recalls visiting Agha's apartment for an executive committee meeting to find that he had been busy on a design project for which layouts were hung on a wire suspended across his huge, two-story living room. (This apartment, in a building next door to Carnegie Hall, had previously been occupied by the great basso Chaliapin. The apartment's second floor had an interior balcony big enough to contain a string quartet.)[28]

In the early 1970s, Agha moved to a farm in Pennsylvania, where his work consisted of occasional consulting jobs and writing. He died in his sleep on May 17, 1978, at the age of eighty-one.

A Man of Order, Taste, and Invention

Though his early years and professional development abroad set Agha apart to a considerable degree from his American colleagues, he had nonetheless a strong sense of the practical which characterized the America of the 1930s. Morrow feels that he would have liked to be remembered "as a man with a fiercely discriminating eye and an absolutely icy kind of reasoning process, because every conclusion he arrived at was based on logic."[29]

Agha delighted in deflating pompous notions about art and design. A popular speaker at conferences and meetings, he made use of his "finely tuned sense of the absurd"[30] both to entertain and to challenge his listeners. His numerous writings are a mine of humorous, acerbic insights into the business of typography, fine arts, and photography. "What is snobbish art scandal today," he wrote, "is an accepted style tomorrow, and a merchandised style the next day."[31] And elsewhere, "Art tendencies come and go and unite with each other, ruled by the law that someone called the law of recurring aesthetic nausea. What is a revolutionary *Putsch* today is an accepted popular style in fifteen years, and an emetic in thirty years from the moment of its inception."[32]

Agha at a favorite pastime, chess. Joyce Morrow Collection, Rochester Institute of Technology.

Color drawing by Agha entitled "One of the latest styles in orthopedic collars." This informal sketch, made for a friend, is representative of Agha's sharp wit. 7¼″ × 10½″.

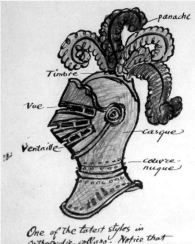

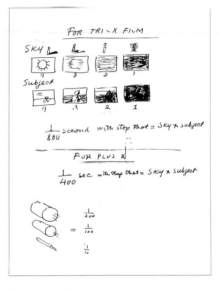

Drawing by Agha for a contest to design a new symbol for the United Nations. 6½″ × 7½″. Joyce Morrow Collection, Rochester Institute of Technology.

Line drawing by Agha, most likely of publisher Alfred Knopf.

Diagram made by Agha as he was teaching someone the fundamentals of photography.

For Agha the best art or design criticism was not a defense of what one liked, but rather a statement describing what made a thing work. Artists and designers were not close to the gods. Their work was less the result of unique inspiration than of life's circumstances and a job's demands. A good example of Agha's particular brand of insight into what made artists tick can be found in a 1932 article on the photographer Ralph Steiner, who had made quite a splash in the art world with his up-angled shots of Manhattan skyscrapers. According to Agha, because Steiner's first photographic period had been spent in New England, a place "entirely devoid of skyscrapers," his second period was "duly marked by the impressions of the first skyscrapers he saw. His natural reaction was to point his Graflex upwards and snap the skyscrapers. Although there was nothing elaborately conscious in this simple action at first, it developed later into a sensation."[33] In short, the tendency of Agha's writings about the nature of art and design was to puncture pretension and to acknowledge the functional, rational basis for the act of designing.

Agha's cynicism extended to his assessment of his own professional accomplishments. The record, however, speaks for itself. His years at Condé Nast shaped the direction of magazine design and, as George Lois has said, "pushed design beyond form and color into the practical world of communication and commerce."[34] Possibly more important was his casting of new definitions for the designer and the art director. The designer became a respected decision maker and the art director an equal to the editor. William Golden, in 1959, recalled that Agha had effected these major changes by "the simple process of demonstrating that the designer could also think."[35]

Agha Chronology

1896
Born in Nikolayev, Russia

1923
Receives diploma from National School of Modern Oriental Languages, Paris

1928
Art director, *Vogue* magazine in Berlin

1929
Emigrates to the United States

1929–1943
Art Director, Condé Nast Publications

1930
Time magazine writes article on Agha

1930
Vogue prints first bleed-edged photograph

1932
First full-color photograph on cover of *Vogue*

1934–1935
President, New York Art Directors Club

1939
"Agha's American Decade," issue of *PM* magazine, devoted to Agha

1943
Leaves Condé Nast Publications, establishes consulting business

1953–1955
President, American Institute of Graphic Arts

1958
Speaker at "Creativity" conference sponsored by Art Directors Club of New York

1978
Dies in Pennsylvania

The man held by many to have been the century's greatest art director was born on a winter day in Russia, in a hunting lodge in the forest between what was then St. Petersburg and the Finnish border.[1] Alexey Brodovitch was the son of aristocratic and wealthy parents. His father, Cheslav, was a military physician, Freudian psychiatrist, and sportsman; his mother was an amateur painter.

In 1905, during the Russo-Japanese War, Brodovitch's father was posted to Moscow as administrator of a hospital for Japanese prisoners. Here began the young Brodovitch's visual education. He was given a box camera and used the hospital and its patients as subject matter. When his mother gave birth to a daughter, the young Alexey was present and photographed the event.

After six months his father was reassigned to St. Petersburg as administrator of a mental institution. Brodovitch was enrolled in one of the most progressive schools in St. Petersburg, the Gymnase Tenichev. On his graduation in 1914 his parents planned to enroll him in the Imperial Art Academy, but the beginning of World War I intervened, and the willful Alexey ran away from home repeatedly to fight in the czar's army.

His leadership ability was recognized, and Brodovitch was sent to officers' school for about four months, before his parents had him returned home. Yielding at last to his obsession with the military, Brodovitch's parents enrolled him in the Corps des Pages, the West Point of czarist Russia, in 1915. After a year he emerged an observant lieutenant, wise in the ways of assessing people and their needs. His first assignment was as a member of the Archtirsky Hussars, a regiment of the Russian Imperial Cavalry to which his relatives had belonged; he was stationed in Rumania, where he became a captain.

By 1918 the civil war was under way. Brodovitch served in the White Army of the czar, not only, as he said, for "political . . . reasons, but to save my own life and the life of my comrades."[2] Having fled from the Bolsheviks in Odessa, a remnant of the White Army escaped to the Caucasus, where a few hundred men with no rifles and only picks for weapons attempted to defend thousands of refugees. Brodovitch's right side was temporarily paralyzed as a result of a wound, and he was removed to a hospital for eight months. It was at this time that he met his future wife, Nina, who drove a wagon carrying wounded soldiers to the hospital.

In 1920, penniless and fleeing for their lives, Nina and Alexey were reunited with his family. With his mother, father, brother, and sister, Brodovitch set sail in a small ship belonging to his father for Egypt and then Greece. The family ended up in Paris, where, after three months, Nina joined them and married Brodovitch.

Paris Years

After only four months in Paris, Brodovitch was designing sets for the Ballet Russe, working with a fellow Russian, Diaghilev. Diaghilev's revolutionary approach to dance, based on principles of asymmetry and continual motion, and his belief in the integration of dance, music, and scene design, together exerted a powerful influence on Brodovitch. The 1920s were an exciting time to be in Paris. Picasso, Derain, and Matisse were also doing work for the ballet. Pavlova and Nijinsky were at their peaks. As an anonymous newcomer, Brodovitch sought work in as many artistic directions as he could find. Soon he was designing porcelain, glass, and textiles for such famous designers as Poiret, Rodier, and Bianchini and making lay-outs for *Cahiers d'Art* and *Arts et Métiers Graphiques.*

Brodovitch was in the perfect environment for beginning a career in the applied arts. The vitality of modernism was all about him, and the quickly chang-

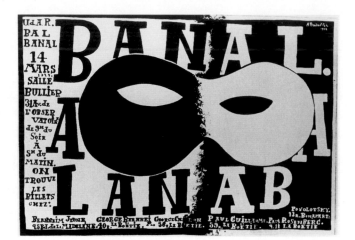

Brodovitch's Bal Banal poster, which launched his career in 1924. The Bal Banal was a benefit dance for Parisian artists. Brodovitch's design won first prize in a competition whose other entrants included Pablo Picasso. The posters were printed in black and white line; colors, in various combinations, were applied by hand in transparent inks.

Bal Banal posters were pasted in irregular patterns on walls throughout Paris. Photograph courtesy Museum of Modern Art.

ing points of view suited perfectly his experimental spirit. Although Art Deco was a prominent style at the time, Brodovitch's work was grounded in a natural antipathy to the ornamental. He seemed able to remain aloof from all but the best of what surrounded him. His work during this period has been called "wry, with a lyrical functionalism that managed never to take itself completely seriously."[3] He knew that the industrial age required a new kind of design.

During 1924 Brodovitch became more involved with graphic design. His interest was enhanced when he won the coveted first prize in a competition to design a poster for Le Bal Banal, a benefit dance for poor artists. Among the recognized artists whom Brodovitch beat out was Pablo Picasso. Winning this prize established Brodovitch as a force in the Paris art and design scene. Over the next five years he designed posters for clients who were receptive to his progressive

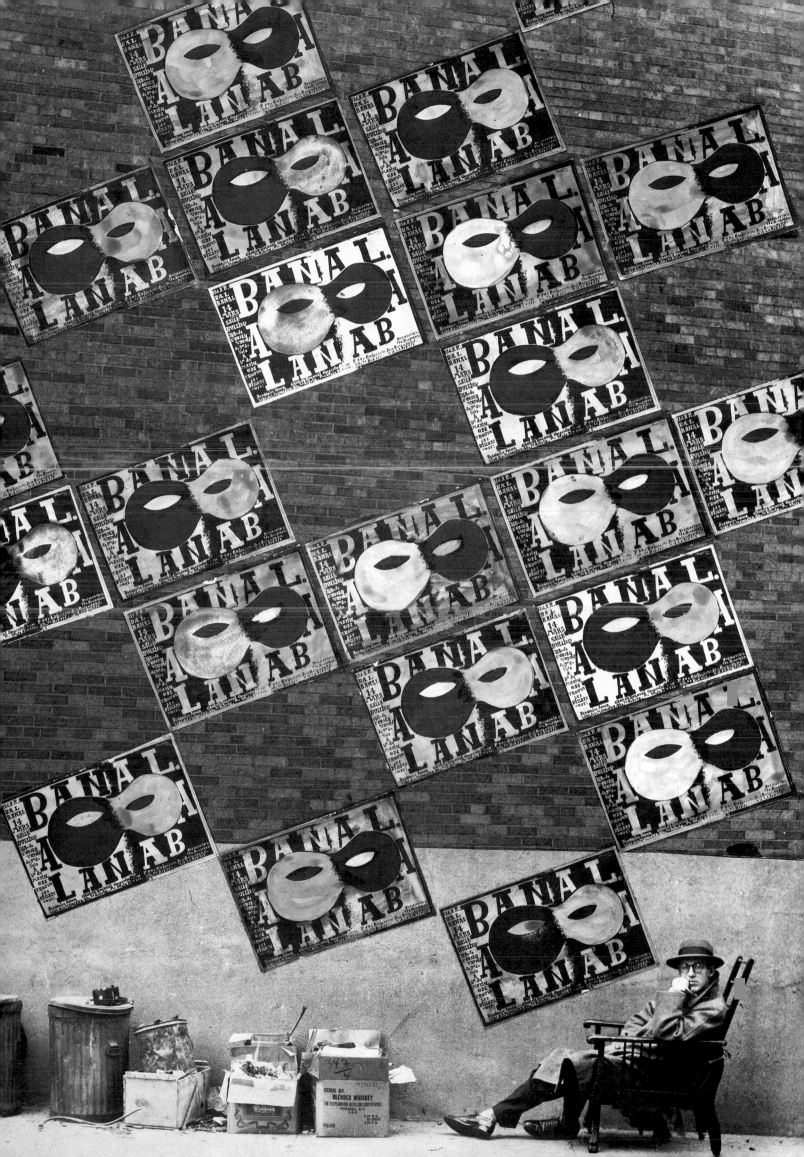

Wall decorations for Maison Prunier, a Paris restaurant. Done in 1927, Brodovitch's work for Prunier's shows the influence of void, form, and shape from Purist painting. His almost pictographic stylization is reminiscent of Léger's figurative treatments. Photograph courtesy Museum of Modern Art.

"Fleurs," 1928. In this cover, Brodovitch's free use of stencil letterforms as part of a pictorial image reflects the typographic influence of the Dada movement. Cover; 9⅝" × 12½".

and experimental graphic concepts. These companies included Martini Vermouth and the stores Le Printemps and Bon Marché. A friend recommended Brodovitch for the job of decorating Prunier's, a seafood restaurant near the Arc de Triomphe. In this project he had the opportunity to apply in a bold fashion what he had been absorbing from the avant-garde artists of his time.

The design for Prunier's was a great success. Brodovitch's professional momentum was sustained by his triumphs at the Paris International Exhibit of the Decorative Arts, where he won two grands prix, two gold medals, and three silver medals for textiles, silver, china, and jewelry. Subsequently he received commissions to decorate the homes of Lucien Lelong, a haut couturier, and Serge Koussevitzky, the conductor.

Brodovitch increasingly specialized in poster design between 1925 and 1930 and devoted himself to experimentation with new techniques with the goal of producing intelligible images through good graphics. By studying both text and typography, he developed a psychological and scientific approach; as the pioneering designers of the Bauhaus and the artists of the Soviet avant-garde had done, he produced posters whose content had been designed to communicate through the arousal of a specific emotional response. He learned how to simplify the subject through analysis of the Purist painters. His posters for Martini, now in the Museum of Modern Art in New York, are among the major products of this fruitful period.

In 1930 Brodovitch was appointed art director at Aux Trois Quartiers, a Paris department store situated on the Place de la Madeleine. He designed a new facade for the store, redid the interior, furnished the third-floor gallery, and designed advertising. As art director for *Arts et Métiers Graphiques* and *Cahiers d'Art*, his designs seemed related to those of Moholy-Nagy and El Lissitzky, in that all three used new techniques beyond drawing and painting for their solutions. During this period Brodovitch also served as art director for Les Magasins Réunis, redesigning their facade. He designed the interior of Studio Athélia, an industrial design firm headed by François Poucet. Brodovitch was also designing and illustrating books by Pushkin and Dostoevsky for the publishing concern Editions de la Pléiade.

Brodovitch Comes to America

In 1928 John Story Jenks, director of the Philadelphia Museum School of Industrial Design (now the Philadelphia College of Art), met Brodovitch in Paris and invited him to create a program in advertising design at the school. Two years later the

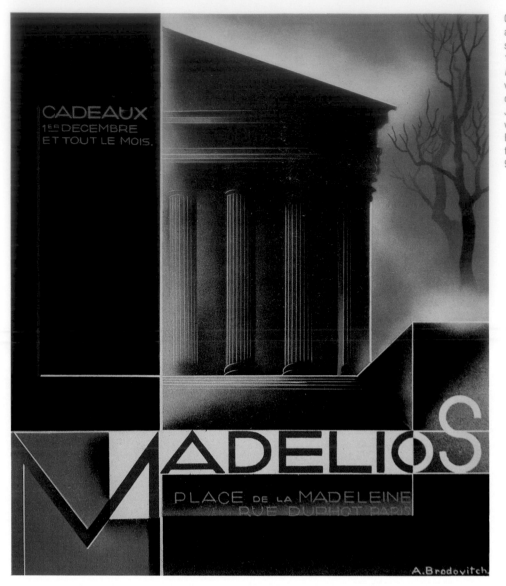

Catalog cover for Madélios, an annex of the Paris department store Aux Trois Quartiers, done in 1928 and printed in *Arts et Métiers Graphiques* magazine, vol. 8. Brodovitch, along with others such as Charles Loupot, Jean Carlu, and A.M. Cassandre, was influenced by the style of French poster art emanating from the Purist movement. 9⅝″ × 12½″.

Catalog cover for Aux Trois Quartiers, reproduced in *Arts et Métiers Graphiques*, vol. 14, November 1929. 9⅝″ × 12½″.

Catalog cover for Aux Trois Quartiers, 1929. Black, yellow, and blue; 9⅝″ × 12½″.

Catalog cover for Athélia, an annex of Aux Trois Quartiers, as reproduced in the November 1929 issue of *Arts et Métiers Graphiques*. Black and white; 9⅝″ × 12½″.

Catalog cover for Madélios, 1929. Color; 9⅝″ × 12½″.

DESIGN LABORATORY
ALEXEY BRODOVITCH

Logo for Brodovitch's design
laboratory.

offer was accepted. From 1930 to 1938 Brodovitch directed the new department;
during most of those years he was also a designer for the N. W. Ayer advertising
agency in Philadelphia.

By 1933, Brodovitch had implemented the first of the design laboratories that
he would conduct for the rest of his career in the United States. The design laboratory was a class for aspiring or already-arrived artists, designers, art directors, professional models, theater people, and photographers. The format was simple:
Brodovitch would present a very open-ended problem for the students, on which
they would work on their own during the time between class meetings, with
subsequent class meetings devoted to discussion of one another's work by the
students, along with Brodovitch's free-flowing criticism of the work—always,
claimed Brodovitch, "from the standpoint of creating a new vision and finding a
personal direction."[4]

Brodovitch's later design laboratories, all conducted in New York City, were
at the New School for Social Research (1941–1949), Richard Avedon's studio
(1947–1949, 1966), the American Institute of Graphic Arts (1964), and the Young and
Rubicam Agency (1964–1965). In addition, he was an instructor of design at
Donnelly Publishers in 1939, a visiting lecturer at Cooper Union and the Pratt Institute in 1940, an instructor in design at the Print Club of Philadelphia from 1946
to 1948, and a visiting critic at the Yale School of Design and Architecture from 1954
to 1957.

Brodovitch's introductory remarks at the opening session of the design laboratory at Young and Rubicam in September 1964 offer an excellent condensation of
his philosophy of education—which he acknowledged to have been largely influenced by the teachings of Krishnamurti, an Indian spiritual leader who had
become known to Westerners through the theosophical movement (they offer, too,
a sample of the English that one former student called "a charming disaster"):

I hope we can discover a new way of communication, how we can invent. Don't
believe that I am a teacher. I am a student—a beginner like you are; I don't think we
can preach or teach. . . . To learn yourself is more difficult than to listen to a teacher.
. . . Please take everything I say with a grain of salt. My way of guiding people is by
irritation. I will try to irritate you, to explore you. . . . If I criticize too much, I will make
a mold of you. You should . . . articulate yourselves.

Dust off tradition. Dust off old habits . . . this will be the first step of our evolution. We must discover new ways of communication. We are to irritate each other.
You should provoke me, and only then can I provoke you back. I believe in this back-
fire technique . . . the more disagreement, the more we learn.

This should be a session of relaxation, not education. We, in our past experi-
ences, are too bound up to think as somebody else taught us. We are here to
doodle and relax.[5]

Brodovitch's open-ended problems were never forgotten by his students. Sam Antiput, who studied with him at Yale in the 1950s, recalls that Brodovitch assigned problems that weren't related to graphic design and that threw students into a turmoil. They would spend as much time trying to figure out what the problem was as trying to solve it. One such problem was "the gas station":

Nobody knew what he meant. This was in the days before the totalitarianism of corporate design, so we didn't know about corporate identity. It was like the blind men and the elephant. Everybody took a different piece of it and got something different out of it. One woman, a textile designer at the Rhode Island School of Design, did uniforms for the gas station attendants. They were not just uniforms, they were functional, with different colors by which you could distinguish who was the manager and who was the mechanic. A couple of people did logos, and one guy who was in love with silk screen did immense signs. I designed a gas station and built a model of it from plexiglass, complete with working electric signs. Two people did oil and gas containers and designed packaging for other products. Brodovitch was the only teacher I ever had who inspired the class by that kind of confusion.[6]

Of the lessons of self-discovery and individuality that Brodovitch taught, Richard Avedon has said, "From Brodovitch you will get no rules or laws. There is nothing you can take away but the essence."[7] Owen Edwards remembers Brodovitch as "one of those rare men who teach, it seems, by their presence alone. An apprentice may sweep the master's floor and even by that act, learn the master's lesson."[8] The list of young talent identified and encouraged by Brodovitch reads like a who's who in visual communication: photographers Richard Avedon, Ted Croner, Irving Penn, Robert Frank, Leslie Gill, Hiro, Art Kane, Sol Mednick, Arnold Newman, Diane Arbus, and Ben Rose; art directors Sam Antiput, Raymond Ballinger, William Bernbach, Bob Cato, Herschel Levitt, Priscilla Peck, Otto Storch, Victor Trasoff, and Henry Wolf; advertising designers Steve Frankfurt, Bob Gage, and Helmut Krone.

Harper's Bazaar

It was as a result of his teaching that Brodovitch came to the attention of Carmel Snow, the new editor of *Harper's Bazaar* magazine. Brodovitch had joined the Art Directors Club and in 1934 was put in charge of hanging one of the club's exhibitions in New York. True to his belief in apprenticeship, he brought some of his students from Philadelphia to help. The innovativeness of the installation intrigued Snow enough to inspire her to offer Brodovitch the position of art director for *Harper's Bazaar*—a position he was to hold for almost twenty-five years.

Brodovitch reluctantly gave up what had become almost a twenty-four-hour-a-day job at the Philadephia College of Art. Once he had agreed to move to Harper's, he used students to prepare an experimental "new look" dummy for the magazine, completing the dummy in a record seventeen days. Throughout his career as an art director he would be known for singling out young people for special assignments and opportunities while most of his contemporaries played it safe by using established, known talent.

At *Harper's Bazaar* Brodovitch was given considerable freedom. He was encouraged to apply new ideas from Europe and to use the magazine as a showcase for young art, design, and photographic talent. His design for the magazine shows the influence of Diaghilev's innovations in ballet, Eisenstein's films, the paintings of Fernand Léger, and Le Corbusier's *Modulor. Junior Bazaar*, which began as a section in the back of *Harper's Bazaar* and eventually became a magazine on its own, offered Brodovitch a setting for his most advanced experimentation. He staffed this project with young people—among them Richard Avedon and Bob Cato—and gave them free rein. Years later, the New York Art Directors Club, in an issue of its *Annual* devoted to Brodovitch, would refer to the Brodovitch years at *Bazaar* as the "Periclean Age."[9]

Brodovitch was able to integrate European sophistication with the dynamic quality of America. Americans were introduced to the images and ideas of Cocteau, Derain, Lurcat, Grosz, Vertes, Fini, Steinberg, Berman, and Topolski. This European contingent was balanced with the powerful American talent of Irving Penn (who had studied with Brodovitch in Philadelphia), Richard Avedon, and Sol Mednick.

The page layouts of *Harper's Bazaar* document the evolution and maturation of Brodovitch's pioneering ideas and sense of orchestration. Allen Hurlburt has said, "Brodovitch brought a rare sense of excitement and clarity to the printed page."[10] He strove to master the integration of text and photography, maintaining the essence of the content with an economy of visual means. The most important of his visual tools was contrast—achieved through dynamic bleeds, cropping, and white space in layouts whose effect is architectonic.

Brodovitch achieved a balance of space and movement through a sensitivity to typography. He regularly used a grouping of four different typefaces, such as Typewriter, Bodoni, Stencil, and a script. Although in most instances he would match the typeface with the feeling inherent in the message, he would freely interrupt this for an appropriate effect and a visual change of pace. His technique included the use of typography to emphasize the shape of the block rather than for legibility; remembering the experiments of his Dada friends in Europe, he would sometimes create free arrangements of type.

Cover for *Harper's Bazaar* magazine, September 1939, with photograph by Leslie Gill. Color. The dimensions of *Harper's Bazaar* throughout Brodovitch's tenure were 9" × 12".

Cover for *Harper's Bazaar*, July 1941, with photograph by Louise Dahl-Wolfe. The use of the Didot Bodoni-like alphabet was an innovation in American graphic design. Color.

Cover for *Junior Bazaar*, April 1946, with photographs by Leslie Gill. Note the integration of the subtle, high-key photographs with flat color shapes and other icons. Brodovitch's *Junior Bazaar* was 9" × 12".

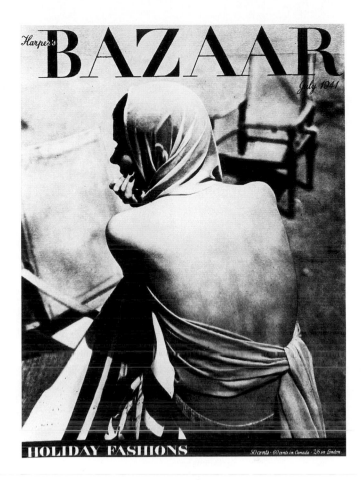

Left: A belted black
topcoat in wool suede
with dropped shoulders.
$49.95. Junior Deb,
at Milgrim. Fitz-William belt.

Left: A squared-off hipcoat
in green shetland wool
with button flaps at
the neck and wrists.
$17.95. Bonwit Teller.

Left: A tailored shirtwaist
dress in dark red wool
jersey, belted in brown
leather. $22.95. Huxley,
at Bloomingdale.

Right: A waterproof
topcoat of bright green
shetland wool with
flap cuffs. $22.95.
Bonwit Teller. Phelps belt.

Right: A black and
blue wool jersey dress.
$16.95. Dartford Deb, in
Alden jersey at Abraham
and Straus, Brooklyn.

Right: A wide skirt of
white wool, striped tan.
$8.95. Jay Originals,
at Arnold Constable.
Add your own jersey.

Left: A wool jersey
shirt and a skirt of kelly
green wool jersey, striped
black. Both by Huxley.
Fitz-William belt.

Left: A dress of
turquoise wool with a tight
buttoned top and a
separate straight-cut skirt.
Ellen Kaye original.

Left: A cotton vest.
$14.95. A black jersey
blouse. $9.95. And a
jersey dirndl. $12.95.
All Tilly Schanzer, at Russeks.

PHOTOGRAPHS BY LESLIE GILL

Two-page layout from the August
1949 *Junior Bazaar*. Brodovitch
used a simple checkerboard idea
on this spread to present fashion
photographs by Leslie Gill. To
emphasize the asymmetric balance of these pages and to interrupt the rhythm, he introduced
globes and books and other elements such as staggered type
lines. Color.

Spread from *Junior Bazaar*, May
1946. Using a photograph by
Richard Avedon, Brodovitch carefully interlocked the elements
necessary for the message.
Color.

BY THE SUN, BY THE AIR, BY THE BEAUTIFUL SEA

In the May 1946 issue of *Junior Bazaar* Brodovitch used a photograph of one of his own low-cost string chairs. He had shown these furniture designs in a competitive exhibition at the Museum of Modern Art in the 1940s. Though Brodovitch is primarily known as a magazine designer and teacher of photography, his interests were not limited to two dimensional design. Black and white.

An associate on the staff at *Bazaar*, Marvin Israel, saw Brodovitch as a man obsessed with change. "Each issue had in some way to be unusual," said Israel; "I think it was a state of perpetual optimism."[11] During the Brodovitch years *Bazaar* was a magnet for the most brilliant minds in visual communications. Its design exerted a great influence on other magazines of the time, particularly *Life* and *Look.* George Bunker characterizes this period as "a time when magazine design was simply decorative in the most banal sense. Brodovitch had the imagination and sensibility to recognize its communication potential."[12]

Other Commissions

Brodovitch's characteristic manner of working was to have several projects going at the same time. During his tenure at *Bazaar*, he was designing textiles, wallpaper, racing cars, porcelain, tennis racquets, and lamps. From 1939 to 1941 he was also art director at Saks Fifth Avenue, and from 1941 to 1943 he held the same position at I. Miller; the force of his passion for new visual idioms raised these fashion centers out of mediocrity. During the 1940s he became interested in industrial design, and in 1945 he designed inexpensive knock-down furniture and even pre-fabricated houses. His chairs, made from plywood and rope, were designed to fold up when not in use. He was awarded third prize in an international competition for low-cost furniture conducted by the Museum of Modern Art in late 1940. He also produced several outstanding advertising campaigns for Elizabeth Arden, Helena Rubenstein, and Steinway. In 1940 a reviewer for *Art and Industry* wrote: "One of Alexey Brodovitch's greatest advantages in his work is his variety of style, a lack of personal style that could label him. Brodovitch's technique might be compared to the playing of a good actor who carries no personal peculiarity or mannerisms from one role to another on the stage."[13]

The Ballet Book

In 1945 Brodovitch produced a book entitled *Ballet*, composed entirely of his own photographs of the Ballet Russe, taken as "souvenirs" during the years 1935 to 1939. These images established a language for expressing motion and speed with the camera. Brodovitch's goal was to capture the essence of the ballet by "shooting backstage using the full effect of the footlights, spotlights, creating an unreal atmosphere of fantasy, certainly not violating the intrinsic nature of ballet, which deals with imagery and music."[14] *Ballet*, which was named Book of the Year by the American Institute of Graphic Arts, was instantly the center of controversy, especially among professional photographers, who tended to react negatively to

Typographic page from *Ballet*, a book published in 1945 with photographs and design by Brodovitch and text by Edwin Denby. This is one of the great pages in the history of graphic design. In it Brodovitch has brought together a series of decorative typefaces and alphabets to designate the ballets included in the book; noteworthy are the careful placement, sizing, and selection of the type. Page dimensions: 11″ × 8½″.

Two sample spreads from *Ballet*, 1945. Black and white. The blurred images, shot at a slow shutter speed, represent a dramatic departure from the then-prevailing custom of capturing moving subjects in crisp detail. *Ballet* inaugurated the blurred-action photography that became especially fashionable in the mid-sixties.

Cover for *US Camera* magazine, 1936. This design shows an early application of a simulated out-of-focus image. Color; 10⅞″ × 11⅜″. Photograph courtesy Museum of Modern Art.

LES NOCES
LES CENT BAISERS
SYMPHONIE FANTASTIQUE
LE TRICORNE
BOUTIQUE FANTASQUE
COTILLION
CHOREARTIUM
SEPTIEME
SYMPHONIE
LE LAC DES CYGNES
LES SYLPHIDES
CONCURRENCE

the frequent use of out-of-focus effects. Brodovitch's images were based on a simple idea antithetical to the prevailing custom of making photographs of moving subjects with a fast shutter speed to capture the subjects in crisp detail. Instead, he shot his ballet photographs with a slow shutter speed, allowing "motion itself to brush over his film."[15]

The first attempts had not been successful. Brodovitch had shot the pictures straight with his 35mm Contax camera; when the frames were enlarged, the images were too coarse. He kept experimenting until he discovered that shooting at the slow shutter speed gave him prints with the right mood and rhythm. With his assistant, Herman Landshoff, Brodovitch spent many hours in the darkroom, working to bring this "accidental" effect under his control. He used chemical reduction if he wanted a thin print. He dodged and burned in, and even went so far as to use an airbrush. It has been said that he had to produce up to fifty prints of a given image to finally arrive at one that was acceptable. Penn considers *Ballet* "one of the most important books on photography ever published, because it 'spat in the face of technique' and pointed out a new way in which photographers could work."[16] Bob Cato, a student of and later assistant to Brodovitch, calls the book "one of the great icons on ballet of our time."[17] More than any other single work, *Ballet* inaugurated the blurred-action photography that characterized the midsixties, as seen in Avedon's *Observations* and Ernst Haas's *Life* magazine spreads, including the well-known article on bullfighting.

Portfolio

Brodovitch designed the short-lived graphic arts magazine *Portfolio* in 1950. It was an expensive, lush, large-format publication. Working with him were co-editors George Rosenthal and Frank Zachary, editor of *Town and Country*. The lavish and extravagant qualities of the three issues of *Portfolio* — excessive production costs brought on its early demise — have never been matched in magazine design. Pages and spreads from *Portfolio* appear as fresh and timeless today as they did thirty-eight years ago. Reading a copy of *Portfolio* is a perceptual experience that lingers in the memory because of the magazine's rhythm, cropping of images, use of color, and unusual graphic arts techniques such as blind embossing.

Portfolio's content reflects the range of Brodovitch's interests. There were profiles on Alexander Calder, Joseph Low, Charles Eames, Isamu Noguchi, and Charles Coiner, among others. In 1969 Allen Hurlburt saw "William Steig's figures from *Portfolio* forecasting the Alka Seltzer commercials of the 'blahs' and the 4½-

Caricature of Brodovitch by Dugo, included in a 1942 issue of *A-D* magazine. The caption identifies Brodovitch as "art director at *Harper's Bazaar* since 1935 and designer for industry."

Double-page spread from *Portfolio* magazine, number 3 (1951). *Portfolio* is widely regarded as Brodovitch's most perfect achievement and the pinnacle of magazine design. This issue featured an article on the American painter Jackson Pollock. In this spread Brodovitch integrated heading type, text type, a close-up view of the artist's work area, and a carefully cropped photograph of the artist, almost falling off the page, in front of one of his paintings. The dramatic blending of copy and photography shows Brodovitch's special skill at magazine page layout. Black and white; 10¾″ × 13″.

Double-page spread from the Jackson Pollock article in *Portfolio* 3. For these pages Brodovitch enlarged several of Pollock's characteristic drip forms to suggest dancing figures.

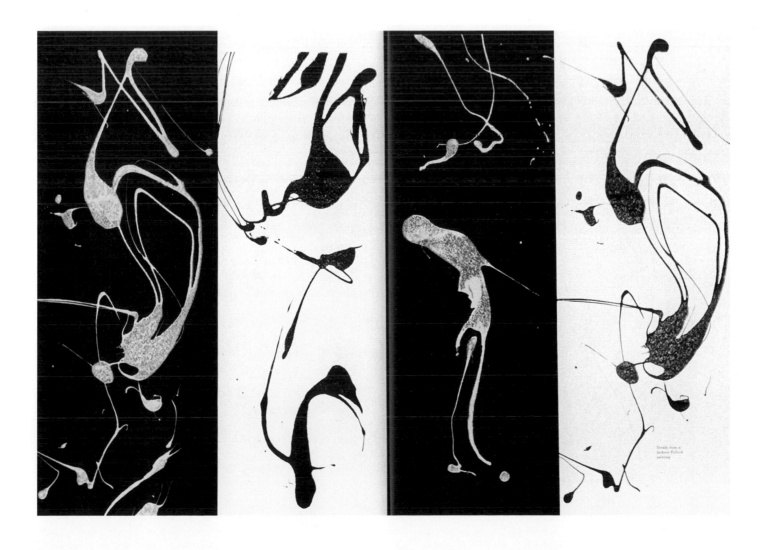

foot foldout on the Mummers parade predicting the psychedelic era of the 1960s."[18] In *Portfolio* Brodovitch had an opportunity to extend and amplify the qualities he had introduced at *Harper's Bazaar*. Freed from the pressures of advertising and responsible to no top-heavy bureaucracy, he could package *Portfolio* the way he wished. Hurlburt calls *Portfolio* "a culmination of the design ideas that had surfaced in the fertile 1920s and 1930s and . . . a forecast of styles to appear in the decades ahead."[19] Ten years later, the arts magazine *Show*, designed by Henry Wolf and published by Huntington Hartford, was a clear example of the Brodovitch influence. Many have characterized *Portfolio* as Brodovitch's most perfect, finished achievement and a landmark in the history of magazine design. "Nobody has really come up with anything either in a book or a magazine that comes close to it," asserts Sam Antiput. "*Portfolio* was enough for one person to have done."[20]

After *Bazaar*

In 1958 Brodovitch was succeeded as art director of *Harper's Bazaar* by Henry Wolf. (Characterizations of his departure range from an amicable resignation to a brutal firing.) He now put his time into book projects and teaching. In collaboration with Richard Avedon and Truman Capote, he produced *Observations* (1959), a visual and verbal look at important personalities of the time. Philip Meggs has called *Observations* "a landmark of book design due to its visual flow and organic layout."[21] In the book Capote offered the following testimonial to his collaborator:

What Dom Perignon was to champagne, Mendel to genetics, so this over-keyed and quietly chaotic but always kindly mannered Russian-born American has been to the art of photographic design and editorial layout, a profession to which he brings boldness bordering on revolution, an eye unexcelled, and in educated terms, a taste for vanguard experiment that has been for thirty-plus years the awe, just possibly the making, of all who have ever had the privilege of his guidance.[22]

Other book design projects of the late 1950s and early 1960s include *Calder* by Pedro Currero, *Salon Society* by David Attie, *Day in Paris* by André Kertesz, and *The World According to Carmel Snow*.

Brodovitch's career ended in 1966. That year, he fell and broke his hip—the last in a lifelong series of catastrophes, both physical and spiritual, that had worn away his stamina. First had come the war wound of 1918. In 1938 his beloved country home in Connecticut had burned to the ground; fires later destroyed his other homes in Phoenixville, Pennsylvania, and Bridgehampton, Long Island. In 1949 he was hit by a truck while crossing the street and spent several months in a hospital as a result. (As fate would have it, the truck belonged to the Hearst Corporation, owner of *Harper's Bazaar* and thus Brodovitch's employer. He was unable to sue or collect damages, lest he jeopardize his job.)

His marriage was another source of sorrow. There were periods of estrangement and discord; both partners drank heavily. Throughout Brodovitch's career, Nina and their son, Nikita, stayed where they were most comfortable — in the country, working the succession of farms the family owned. Both Brodovitch and his wife had an abiding love for animals, particularly horses, and the farms always had a complement of livestock. The marriage, despite its difficulties, lasted for forty years until Nina's third and fatal heart attack in 1959. Her death inaugurated for Brodovitch a series of hospitalizations for acute depression.

In 1967, in frail health, realizing that his teaching and designing career was over, Brodovitch packed his possessions, gave his work to Mildred Constantine of the Museum of Modern Art, and retired to the south of France. He and his wife had purchased an old olive mill in Oppède-les-Vieux some years before, and the mill was his home until the steepness of the town's hills and the weakness of his hip forced him to move to another community, Le Thor. There he died on April 15, 1971, destitute and all but forgotten.

A New Way of Communication

In both his teaching and his work as a designer, Alexey Brodovitch was concerned with discovering the essences of things — with finding and expressing what Otto Storch called "the rightfulness of the idea."[23] Though never entirely comfortable in the commercial world, he was generally able to win reluctant clients over to a design solution because of the convincing rightness of that solution. Brodovitch's graphics seem to touch viewers more deeply than do most. A perfectionist when it came to craftsmanship, he insisted nonetheless that structure should not be seen but felt. Technique, he said, is only a means to an end. When it becomes an end in itself, the result is often cliché. Brodovitch would not stand for mediocrity in any form. He demanded that those who worked for him constantly guard against anything but their finest performance.

European artists were used to demanding the right to the concept and the entire finished execution. While others such as Cassandre and Carlu found working in America with its division of labor difficult, Brodovitch's patience and good salesmanship, his genuine feeling of responsibility to his clients, and most of all his conviction of his own authority enabled him to preserve the control he wanted over his projects.

Double-page spread from *Observations* (1959), a book designed by Brodovitch, with text by Truman Capote and photographs by Richard Avedon. This presentation of repeated high-contrast images of dancing figures (taken from the musical comedy *The Pajama Game*) captures the feeling of movement on the printed page. Black and white. Page dimensions: 10½″ × 14⁵⁄₁₆″ Photograph © 1954 by Richard Avedon Inc. All rights reserved.

Cover of *Observations*. Color. Photograph courtesy Museum of Modern Art.

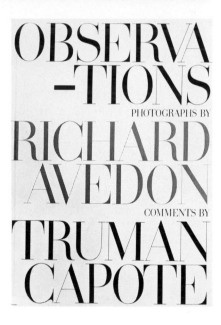

Brodovitch's page layouts demonstrate a bold approach to the integration of visual elements—white space, art, and typography—and the integration of these, in turn, with the idea in the text. His goal was an aesthetic unity that was elegant yet fluid. "There is no recipe for good layout," he said; "but what must be maintained is a feeling of change and contrast."[24] His pages conveyed the message with the fewest possible elements. He gave first priority to the text placement and then followed with the other parts of the story. He sometimes arranged the photostats and type proofs and kept them in place under a sheet of glass until the final layout appeared. Francis McFadden remembers that "it was a pleasure to watch him at work. He was so swift and so sure . . . his speed was dazzling. A quick slash or two on the cutting board, a minute's juggling of the photostats, a slather of art gum, and the required pages were complete."[25] His page layouts showed an abundance of white space, which caused much despair among the copywriters.

More dramatic was his technique of planning the pages in a linear sequence to enhance the flow of the magazine. He would place a long line of eighty pages in

Page from *Observations*. The book contained photographic portraits of famous people by Richard Avedon with comments by Truman Capote. This page, with Capote's tribute to Brodovitch, shows the designer walking around page spreads from the book, which had been placed on the floor so that he could see the rhythm evident in the sequencing of the images. This technique, which Brodovitch also used for laying out magazines, provided a "holistic" sense of the book's design. Black and white. Photograph © 1959 by Richard Avedon Inc. All rights reserved.

Above: the man responsible for the design of this book: Alexey Brodovitch. What Dom Perignon was to champagne, Mendel to genetics, so this over-keyed and quietly chaotic but always kindly mannered Russian-born American has been to the art of photographic design and editorial lay-out, a profession to which he brings boldness bordering on revolution, an eye unexcelled, and, in educated terms, a taste for vanguard experiment that has been for thirty-plus years the awe, just possibly the making, of all who have ever had the privilege of his guidance.

Alexey Brodovitch. Photograph by
Richard Avedon, taken in 1969 at
Le Thor, France. © 1969 by
Richard Avedon Inc. All rights
reserved.

Poster by Marvin Israel announcing the posthumous exhibition
"Hommage à Alexey Brodovitch"
at the Grand Palais in Paris in
1982. Color; 45¼" × 29⅞".
© 1982 by the Estate of Marvin
Israel. All rights reserved.

a row on the floor, so that he could see the magazine as an entity rather than just spreads. (Avedon recollects that Brodovitch attributed his sense of magazine flow to his study of Corbusier's *Modulor*.) Each issue of the magazine was built with concern for the integrity of the individual page, the spread, and the overall pacing of the pages.

Brodovitch could make an effective layout using unexciting photographs. He said, "A layout man should be simple with good photographs. He should perform acrobatics when the pictures are bad."[26] He was a master at cropping photographs, at enlarging and otherwise altering photographic images, and at juxtaposing them. And he had an uncanny ability to select outstanding images from contact sheets.

Boredom, said Brodovitch, is the sickness of our time. His way of combatting it was through invention and the element of surprise — which latter, he felt, was the major asset of the visual communicator. For Brodovitch the good photographer or designer "must be two persons in one — a magician and a psychologist. In a highly competitive field he must always be able to pull new pictures, like rabbits, out of his hat. And as a psychologist, he had the job of searching to capture what is unexpected and new."[27]

Brodovitch succeeded not only in finding new ways to communicate but also in training many of the leading members of the next generation of graphic designers and photographers to find their own ways. It is true that he was very sparing in words of praise for students or colleagues; many found him cold and aloof. Henry Wolf, his successor at *Bazaar*, felt that the enigmatic and impenetrable air of tragedy that surrounded him generated a desire to please and help him, to relieve his discomfort by bringing him, like an offering, the best work one was capable of producing. The wish to reach him, to connect somehow with this gentle but always distant man, was never entirely satisfied. "No two people of those who knew him, knew him the same way," concludes Richard Avedon. "Brodovitch the man will not stand clear."[28] What is abundantly clear, though, is the fundamental importance of his work. Irving Penn has said, "All designers, all photographers, all art directors whether they know it or not are students of Alexey Brodovitch."[29]

Brodovitch Chronology

1898
Born in Ogolitchi, Russia

1914–1915
Student at Gymnase Tenichev, St. Petersburg

1915–1916
Enrolled in Corps des Pages military academy, St. Petersburg

1916–1918
Captain in the Twelfth Archtirsky Hussars of the Russian Imperial Cavalry

1920–1926
Scenery designer for Diaghilev's Ballet Russe and designer of furnishings, books, and posters in Paris

1924
First prize, Bal Banal poster competition, Paris

1928
Art director, Aux Trois Quartiers, Paris

1930–1938
Director of Advertising Arts Department, Philadelphia Museum School of Industrial Art

1931–1938
Designer, N. W. Ayer, Philadelphia and New York

1934–1958
Art director, *Harper's Bazaar* magazine

1939–1941
Art director, Saks Fifth Avenue, New York, New York

1941–1943
Art director, I. Miller and Sons, New York, New York

1941–1949
Instructor, Brodovitch Design Laboratory, New School for Social Research, New York, New York

1945
Book of the Year Award, American Institute of Graphic Arts, for *Ballet*

1949–1951
Art director, *Portfolio* magazine

1954–1957
Visiting critic, Yale University School of Design and Architecture

1967
Retires to Oppède-les-Vieux, France

1969
Moves to Le Thor, France

1971
Dies in Le Thor

1972
Inducted into Hall of Fame of the New York Art Directors Club

1972
Posthumous exhibit, "Alexey Brodovitch and His Influence," Philadelphia College of Art

Charles Coiner 1898–

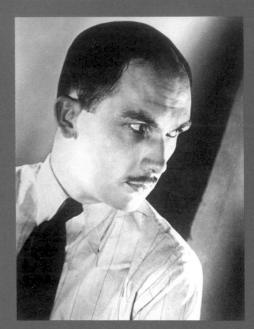

The year that Charles Toucey Coiner was born in Santa Barbara, California, to Charles Anderson Coiner and Mary Gascoigne Coiner, the N. W. Ayer and Son advertising agency a continent away hired its first commercial artist to help with copy preparation. At seventeen, Coiner decided to become a commercial artist and went to work as a section hand on the Southern Pacific Railway to earn the money he would need for his education. At nineteen he arrived in Chicago to study commercial art at the Chicago Academy of Fine Arts; he also took classes at the Art Institute of Chicago. After a year at the Academy, he joined the Chicago office of Erwin and Wasey, a nationwide advertising agency, in 1919. The six years he spent in the art department there, though largely uneventful, provided him with a solid foundation for the rest of his career.

Coiner's coming of age in the field of advertising design coincided with a movement on the part of a few select clients to embrace modernism in their advertising. These clients were predominantly makers of luxury products such as jewelry, automobiles, and perfumes, although a few enlightened producers of industrial products such as pistons, roller bearings, and batteries came along for the ride. By 1928 Herbert Kerkow was reporting that "American advertising art has gone modernistic"; two years later Brenda Ueland wrote in the *Saturday Evening Post*, "You will need to know about Cézanne, Gauguin, and Matisse [because] Buckeye Art is now out."[1] American businesses were becoming cautiously interested in the art of the European avant garde, because its dramatic newness brought attention to their products. Modernism offered a new visual vocabulary to the American corporation, through which it could become a "patron" of the arts.

In 1924 Charles Coiner was caught up in this rush to modernism when he moved to Philadelphia to join the art department at N. W. Ayer. Coiner's love for modern art was self-taught and self-inspired. N. W. Ayer was—along with Erwin and Wasey, Calkins and Holden, and J. Walter Thompson—at the forefront of agencies that aggressively used modern art in their advertising campaigns. America's oldest advertising firm, Ayer had always been a pioneering organization and had appointed staff art directors as early as 1910.[2] As a matter of corporate policy, accounts were distributed among all fields of advertising, even at the cost of turning down very large new accounts that might upset this special "balance." The company was represented in all but two of the twenty-three major classes of advertising accounts. In spite of this prudent, pragmatic organizational stance, Ayer quickly developed a reputation for doing quite contemporary and original work. With Coiner, they employed Norman Kent, Edward Ulreich, Hugh Ferriss, and the

famous photographer Anton Bruehl. Ayer for years had run a remarkable series of
ads for Steinway pianos for which they hired outstanding artists. Steinway, during
this period, paid the unheard-of price of $25,000 for a portrait of Ignace Paderewski
by the Spanish artist Zuloaga. This fee brought the client considerable publicity,
free of charge.

During the mid-1920s an advertising staffer remarked, "Great paintings have
the most irresistible form of salesmanship that has ever been created. To accept
an advertising commission for a really good painter, and to buy the work of a famous
painter, is certainly the surest way to greater returns for the manufacturer."[3] Ayer
clients received forty-one awards during the first nineteen years of exhibitions by
art directors, outdistancing the next competitor by three to one. Ayer pioneered the
production of "beautiful" ads through campaigns for Cannon Mills, Caterpillar
Tractor, Climax Molybdenum, French Line, Marcus Jewelers, DeBeers Diamonds,

An elegant advertisement for Lincoln automobiles from the 1930s. Detailed illustration and the clean typographic area are combined to communicate information about the precision, high-quality product to an affluent audience. 11½" × 14".

This 8½" × 11" magazine ad for the Climax Molybdenum Company, designed by Alexey Brodovitch, shows a progressive approach for 1935. Simple geometric forms symbolize and energize a dull industrial product. The integration of the word "Moly" as part of both the illustration and the headline copy unifies the ad. Coiner was able to bring talented European designers to work for American companies.

and Capehart. "Ayer was perfect for me," Charles Coiner remembers, "because
they supported all the ideas I had."[4] The DeBeers campaign was a noteworthy one
from that period. Rather than using literal photographs of diamonds in the ads,
paintings were used to establish a feeling of romance and distinctiveness by association with fine art. DeBeers sales, which were on a decline when the ads began in
1939, increased twofold with the new campaign. Other important accounts that
Coiner directed were for Lincoln and Ford automobiles.

Coiner's Blue Eagle

Charles Coiner was a dashing figure and very visible in the world of advertising
art in the 1920s and the 1930s. In the depths of the Great Depression, with over
15 million Americans out of work, Coiner was tapped to design a symbol for the
National Recovery Administration (NRA), the federal agency created to encourage

Magazine ad for DeBeers Consolidated Mines, done at N.W. Ayer. The illustration, by Jean Hugo, is called "Honeymoon in Paris." 11" × 14¼".

House advertisement for N.W. Ayer from the 1940s. This ad indicates Ayer's emphasis on a high-quality copywriting approach. The copy concludes with, "advertising will push back the fence rows of business and lead, steadily and surely, into broader fields." 11" × 14½".

Magazine ad for DeBeers Consolidated Mines. With the photography of the young Irving Penn, this ad brings a quality of natural elegance to the promotion of the high-priced product. 11" × 14¼".

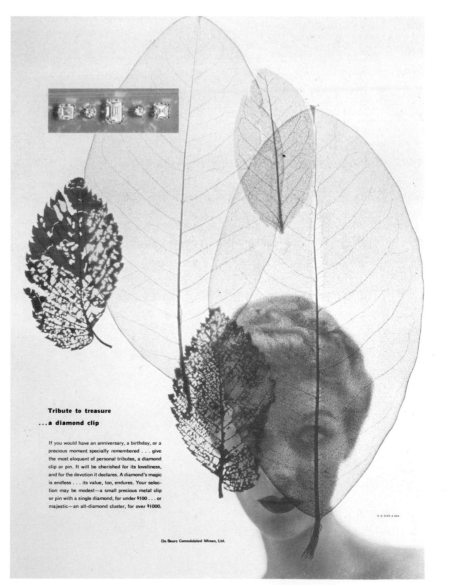

Pencil sketches for the NRA Blue
Eagle symbol, 1933.

Watercolor sketch for the
National Recovery Administration (NRA) Blue Eagle symbol,
done in 1933. 12″ × 15″. Coiner
was among the first prominent
American designers to contribute time and talent in the
service of the federal
government.

Coiner in 1933, at work on the design of the Blue Eagle.

Poster for the NRA, 1934.
12″ × 15″.

industrial recovery and combat unemployment. The design was conceived on June 16, 1933, on an airplane flight to Washington, D.C. Coiner recalls:

I was doodling on a sketch pad and came up with the idea of an eagle, which seemed proper as a patriotic symbol. So when I got there I sat down at a desk and sketched it out. To get some animation, I added a cog in one talon and a sheaf of wheat in the other. I showed it to Johnson [General Hugh S. Johnson, commander in chief of the NRA], who told me, "Get that wheat out of there. This isn't an agricultural program!" I rushed back to the desk and traced it over, substituting lightning bolts for the wheat.[5]

The design was quickly adopted. Displayed—in the form of stickers and window cards—by businesses as an emblem of NRA participation, the Blue Eagle, as it was called, became a household word.

The universal recognition so rapidly gained by the Blue Eagle was helped along by a tireless promotional campaign on the part of General Johnson, who understood that the success of the NRA would rest on its being widely advertised. Between July and October 1933 a flurry of articles with headings like "Employers Swarm to Blue Eagle," "Blue NRA Eagle Drawn by Artist on Plane," "Blue Eagle Design on Business Badge of Honor Drawn in Air," appeared in the nation's newspapers, from the Eureka, California, *Standard* to the Omaha *World Herald* to the Philadelphia *Inquirer.* And in its short life of just under two years, the NRA accomplished remarkable things: some 400 industrial codes of fair practice were signed, covering 20,000,000 of the country's workers and putting 2,785,000 people back to work, adding 3 billion dollars to the nation's payroll.

The publicity for his Blue Eagle made Coiner himself a celebrity. His movie-star good looks graced the photographs that accompanied articles on the NRA. He got letters from long-lost acquaintances and perfect strangers. "My dear Mr. Coiner," wrote a woman from Arden, Oklahoma, "I have a daughter, age seventeen, who does drawing like you. We saw your picture of the eagle and read about you in the newspapers. . . . [My daughter] is a pretty girl and sweet as she can be. Are you married? You see, I am a widow, and she will be looking for a 'connection' real soon."[6] A classmate of Coiner's at Santa Barbara High School wrote, "Just the other day I was wondering where you were and a few days later I saw your picture in the paper as being the originator of the N.R.A. emblem. Good work, Charles. . . . It shows the character of students dear Old Santa Barbara High could turn out, that is, in some instances."[7] A naturalist from Connecticut, after expatiating at length upon the genus *Aquila* and the characteristics of its various species, concluded, "While I appreciate the noble purpose to which this design is to be put, and while it may be that our esteemed President and associates approved of this eagle, I am afraid you are going to have a little difficulty with eagle fanciers. What kind of an eagle is it?"[8]

Back at N. W. Ayer, Coiner continued to produce strikingly modern advertising campaigns in the mid-1930s. A 1950 article on Coiner would characterize his layouts as "distinguished by a freshness of design and originality of conception that owes much to modern art."[9]

CCA and the "Great Ideas"

A most fortunate confluence of people and ideas was the long association of N. W. Ayer and Charles Coiner with the Container Corporation of America (CCA) and its president, Walter Paepcke, that began in 1936. This relationship produced a landmark series of advertising campaigns in which Coiner was afforded an environment particularly conducive to progressive art direction.

CCA had come into being in the 1920s when Walter Paepcke had taken over his father's small Chicago paperboard manufacturing firm and undertaken to give it a national identity. In the twenties the nature of the relationship between industry and the world of advertising art was changing. Business leaders began to be aware of the benefits that artists and designers could provide them. New eye-catching package design, striking architecture, and memorable advertising were indicators of this change. It became fashionable to appear modern. And the European avant-garde provided the visual grammar for this new look.

Paepcke was an enlightened industrialist and a man of ideas. He was later to found the Aspen Institute of Humanistic Studies as a part of the revival of Aspen, Colorado. He supported Mortimer Adler and Robert Hutchins in the Great Books of the Western World project at the University of Chicago. For Coiner, the art director for the CCA account, Paepcke was an ideal client.

A black-and-white ad for the Container Corporation of America, designed by the noted French poster artist A.M. Cassandre with art direction by Charles Coiner. This 1938 ad, targeted at the packaging industry, shows Cassandre's unique ability to focus the reader on a coherent set of icons that reinforce the copy message. 9" × 12¾".

In 1936 the Container Corporation of America was prepared to embrace a new direction for its advertising. Paepcke, together with other company officers and Coiner, evolved a plan: instead of concentrating on CCA's products, the advertising campaign would establish images and associations in the mind of the public through references to noble institutions and ideas of Western culture. Over the life of this campaign, which continued until 1960, several themes were explored, including the United Nations, the United States, and eventually the Great Ideas of Western Man.

The Great Ideas ads for CCA were developed according to a process that began with a small committee of people: members of the company, Mrs. Paepcke, and Charles Coiner. This group selected the statements and quotes. Coiner then visited artists all over the world to find appropriate talent. Once an artist was chosen, Coiner's directions always included the phrase, "We don't want you to do this literally." Final production was accomplished by the design staff at N. W. Ayer under Egbert Jacobsen, then manager of design at CCA. The series, unique in the history of advertising and design, won high praise for both Coiner and CCA. It was

This magazine advertisement for the Container Corporation of America, with an illustration by Jerome Snyder, was done in the 1940s. Coiner, as the representative of CCA's advertising agency, N.W. Ayer, coordinated its ads, in which he presented many of the finest European and American artists and designers to the American public. 8¾" × 11¾".

NEW YORK — *annual purchases: $7¾ billion — mostly packaged.*

CONTAINER CORPORATION OF AMERICA   Save Waste Paper

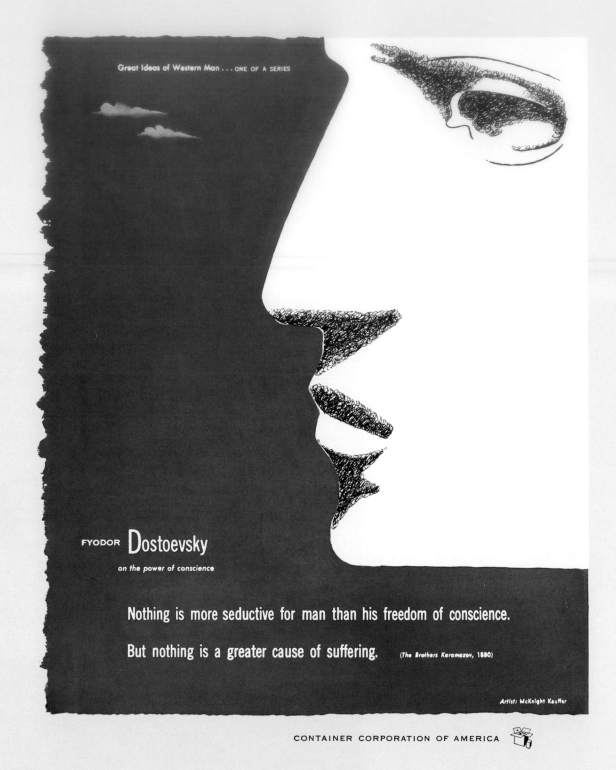

Great Ideas of Western Man . . . ONE OF A SERIES

FYODOR **Dostoevsky**

on the power of conscience

Nothing is more seductive for man than his freedom of conscience.

But nothing is a greater cause of suffering.   *(The Brothers Karamazov, 1880)*

Artist: McKnight Kauffer

CONTAINER CORPORATION OF AMERICA

Magazine ad from 1953, part of CCA's "Great Ideas of Western Man" series. Coiner selected the famous American poster artist E. McKnight Kauffer to design this memorable visual statement.

Designed by Walter Allner, this color ad in CCA's "Great Ideas of Western Man" series shows the power of symbolic shapes, calligraphy, and typography combined into an integrated message. 8½″ × 11″.

as though "a new kind of corporate art patron had emerged."[10] Herbert Bayer would later assert that the Great Ideas campaign established CCA as "an industry leader in identifying itself with the best in design and aesthetics internationally."[11]

As to the relevance of the Great Idea advertisements to his company's enterprise, Walter Paepcke commented, at the end of the first decade of the campaign:

Does it sell boxes? The answer to this is, the direct sale of boxes is not and never has been the purpose of our institutional advertising. But insofar as it creates an acute awareness of our company, giving it a distinctive personality and identifying it with the best in graphic arts, it succeeds extremely well. It is difficult to check the amount of discussion actually stimulated by the "Great Ideas" ads. It must suffice to say that public response is continuous and indicates that the statements do stimulate much thinking. Furthermore, when people say we are helping to promote good citizenship, we know that campaign is good advertising.[12]

In fact, the campaign did sell boxes. CCA's sales increased from 22 million in 1936 to 131 million in 1948.

Bringing Fine Art to Advertising

Charles Coiner became "a midwife to the birth of modern industrial patronage"; his work has been credited with starting a "new cosmopolitanism" in American advertising art.[13] In addition to using the latest techniques in printing and merchandising, Coiner employed, on a free-lance basis, more than a hundred artists over the years, including Sasha Maurer, Alexey Brodovitch, E. McKnight Kauffer, Otto Kuhler, Ludwig Kozma, Josef Binder, Julius Klinger, Otis Shepard, and Frederick Kiesler. He placed his advertisements in "quality" publications that appealed to a sophisticated readership.

During this period Coiner wrote several essays for *Advertising Arts.* In one of these, referring to the European avant-garde, he said, "It would seem rather a bold stroke to employ such artists, yet France was the source of virtually all that is new and significant in art."[14] Coiner was an active supporter of other American designers—such as M. F. Agha, John Averill, Lester Beall, Alexey Brodovitch, Lucille Corcos, William Golden, Cipe Pineles, and Leo Rackow—who were finding a new direction in modernism.

Coiner reveled in his dealings with artists. He was on the pier waiting for the boat that brought A. M. Cassandre, the famous poster artist, to America. In his pocket was a contract, which he got Cassandre to sign before they left the pier, thus commissioning him to design the first in the new series of ads for the Container Corporation of America. Other emigrés who worked for the campaign were Toni Zepf, Herbert Matter, Gyorgy Kepes, Fernand Léger, Jean Carlu, and Herbert Bayer.

Bayer, who had worked in Berlin in the 1920s and 1930s, was the most distinguished advertising artist in Europe.

As art director for Ayer's Dole Pineapple account, Coiner sent Isamu Noguchi, Georgia O'Keeffe, and Pierre Roy to Hawaii to do ads that stressed the romantic aspect of the fruit. The Dole Pineapple campaign also featured the work of A. M. Cassandre. Artists such as Dufy, Picasso, Derain, and Covarrubias produced work for the DeBeers Diamond ads, designed by Paul Darrow. Advocate though he was of the employment of these artists in advertising, Coiner was quick to express concern about the indiscriminate use of modern art: "The only test of any advertising design is: Will it put over the advertiser's story or sell his product? Fine art may sell cardboard containers and diamonds under certain circumstances, but that does not mean it will sell soft drinks or cigarettes."[15]

Government Design During World War II

While actively involved in his many advertising accounts at N. W. Ayer, Coiner also undertook major design projects for the government. In 1939, with World War II under way in Europe, he designed an extensive program of symbols for the United States Citizens' Defense Corps (CDC), later to be called Civil Defense (CD). This was a fully systematized plan for a series of graphic marks for different aspects of the defense program on the home front. Had there been war on the United States mainland, these symbols would have assisted ambulance drivers, messengers, rescue squads, auxiliary police, and others. The symbol program anticipated by thirty years the development of corporate identity standards programs.

In 1940 Coiner was appointed art consultant to the Office of Emergency Management, which put to work many of America's top designers. Among his contributions were propaganda posters for the war industries. "When I started the government work," Coiner recalls, "people were not conscious of the fact that we were about ready to go into war. We had to get workers steamed up, and a lot of the posters were made for that purpose."[16] This work included supervising the famous "Production" poster, designed by the French artist Jean Carlu.

During the war, Coiner was art director on an advertising campaign for Boeing, a large supplier of aircraft for the government. His idea with these ads was to make them look like news and information, and not like ads. This series was one of Coiner's most successful.

Color magazine ad for the Dole Pineapple account, September 1938. Coiner commissioned A.M. Cassandre to produce this ad, which makes use of semi-abstract imagery—unusual in advertising at the time. 9½" × 13".

The Postwar Years

In 1950 the experimental magazine *Portfolio*, edited by Frank Zachary and designed by Alexey Brodovitch, ran an extensive profile article on Charles Coiner. "As art director for N. W. Ayer," the article explained, "Charles Coiner serves sixty major clients who buy seventy million dollars worth of advertising space annually to promote their wares, which range from airplanes to automobiles and soup to suspenders." Coiner, always the optimist, was quoted as announcing that the American public was "becoming acutely design conscious. It expects everything from locomotives to coffee cups to have pleasing functional shapes."[17]

Coiner's assessment of the degree of development of American taste—at least, of that taste as reflected by N. W. Ayer's clients' demands—was not to be borne out by reality. Primarily a print-oriented designer, he struggled with the changes in the advertising business as photography and television began to dominate the late 1950s. He acknowledged reluctantly that demonstrating the product as a selling technique is hard to beat. By 1960, change was very much in the air. Walter Paepcke died that year. Herbert Bayer left the Container Corporation of America, and in 1964—forty years after he had joined the firm—Charles Coiner retired from N. W. Ayer.

At his beautiful Coltsfoot Farm in Bucks County, Pennsylvania, Coiner returned to what he calls his two main interests in life, the study of nature and painting. Nature, he says, provides him with "an inexhaustible source of inspiration and a timely subject, too, in that there is currently too much man-made disarrangement and disharmony in the development of our remaining open spaces. Why perpetuate it on canvas? Better, it seems to me, to show the unspoiled places left in the world. There is a great and growing need for tranquility in every one of us."[18]

The Art Director's Art Director

Throughout his long years as art director and consultant, Coiner witnessed what he called the American people's war on ugliness. He saw business and industry turning increasingly to artists to be footsoldiers in that war, yet many artists were drawing fastidiously away, unwilling to prostitute their art. Coiner believed that art schools were responsible for the low esteem in which commercial work was held—an attitude he considered "mischievous nonsense."

If the industrial designer is prostituting his art, then so was the cave man who made records of hunting, the Egyptian who adapted himself to the decorative needs of his time, the Pompeiian who fashioned exquisite and useful objects in

Drawings from Coiner's sketchbook for several of the government graphic design projects he undertook during World War II. This page was reproduced in a major article on Coiner in Alexey Brodovitch's *Portfolio* magazine in 1950. 10¾" × 13".

Magazine advertisement for Boeing produced during World War II. To this series, run in black and white, Coiner imparted a documentary, "news"-like character. 11½" × 13½".

Page of color cuts for Coiner's National War Fund symbol, 1943. This symbol was applied to some 132,000,000 pieces of literature put out by war relief agencies. Coiner was an early proponent of systematic identity programs for organizations.

Coiner studying the famous "Production" poster by Jean Carlu. As a volunteer consultant to the U.S. government during World War II, Coiner brought famous European designers in to do propaganda pieces encouraging participation in the war effort. This poster, with its powerful illustration and related typography, is a masterpiece in the history of graphic design.

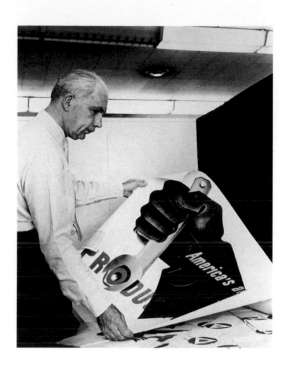

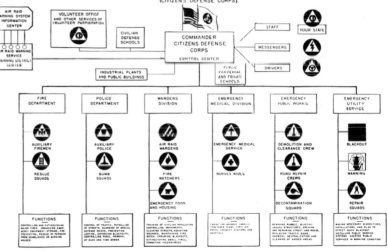

CIVILIAN PROTECTION ORGANIZATION FOR A MUNICIPALITY
(CITIZEN'S DEFENSE CORPS)

Coiner designed the symbols for the U.S. government's Citizens' Defense Corps during World War II — an important early example of a systematic identity program. This diagram sets forth the organization of the symbols in the system.

metal and clay, the Italians who were commissioned by royal families to cover cathedral walls with fresco . . . and to narrow the comparison to one man, so must Michelangelo have prostituted his art when he designed the uniforms of the Swiss Guards...and executed the tombs of the Medici.[19]

Coiner believed that a partnership between artists and industry was needed. "Industry should have a greater recognition of the rare talent and display more guts in putting it to use. The independent designer, however, could make a more serious effort to work with industry. He must put aside the 'precious' attitude about his work and learn to cooperate in joint effort."[20]

Coiner himself had a rare gift for cooperation in his advertising work. When his accomplishments are discussed, he always gives away the credit to others on his staff. He was a true team player with his creative group at N. W. Ayer, where his value was in giving a suggestion here, applying the brakes there, and coordinating all ideas in harmony with the overall plan for each account. He was well known in the business for his "deft courage" in selecting staff members — his ability to see the potential in inexperienced young designers. Coiner would hire young people right out of art school and train them within the department. "The fun of this business," he once said, "is developing people."[21] Robert Bach, in his speech welcoming Coiner into the Art Directors Hall of Fame, remarked,

He had a genius for spotting talent and bringing it into a climate which encouraged creative growth. "Coiner's Men," as his staff was called, stayed on at N. W. Ayer much longer than usual and were consistent in refusing better offers to move upward in the business. They were confident in always having Coiner's backing and therefore had a freedom to accomplish brilliant work.[22]

In the course of his career, Charles Coiner achieved many firsts. He introduced foreign artists to the American public to a greater extent than did any other art director. He was the first major art director to bridge the gap between fine art and applied art. He was the first major American graphic designer to contribute his talents to government projects. And he achieved a place for the art director as a prominent member of the problem-solving team.

Coiner Chronology

1898
Born in Santa Barbara, California

1917–1919
Studies at Chicago Academy of Fine Arts and Art Institute of Chicago

1919–1924
Designer at Erwin and Wasey, Chicago

1924
Joins N. W. Ayer and Son, Philadelphia

1924
Buys Coltsfoot Farm, near Philadelphia

1929
Named art director at N. W. Ayer

1933
Designs "Blue Eagle" symbol for National Recovery Administration

1936
Named vice-president, N. W. Ayer

1939
Designs symbol program for U.S. Citizens' Defense Corps

1949
First American to receive Art Director of the Year award from the National Society of Art Directors

1949
Named to Art Directors Hall of Fame

1964
Retires from N. W. Ayer

1986
Exhibition of paintings at Midtown Gallery, New York, New York

William Golden 1911–1959

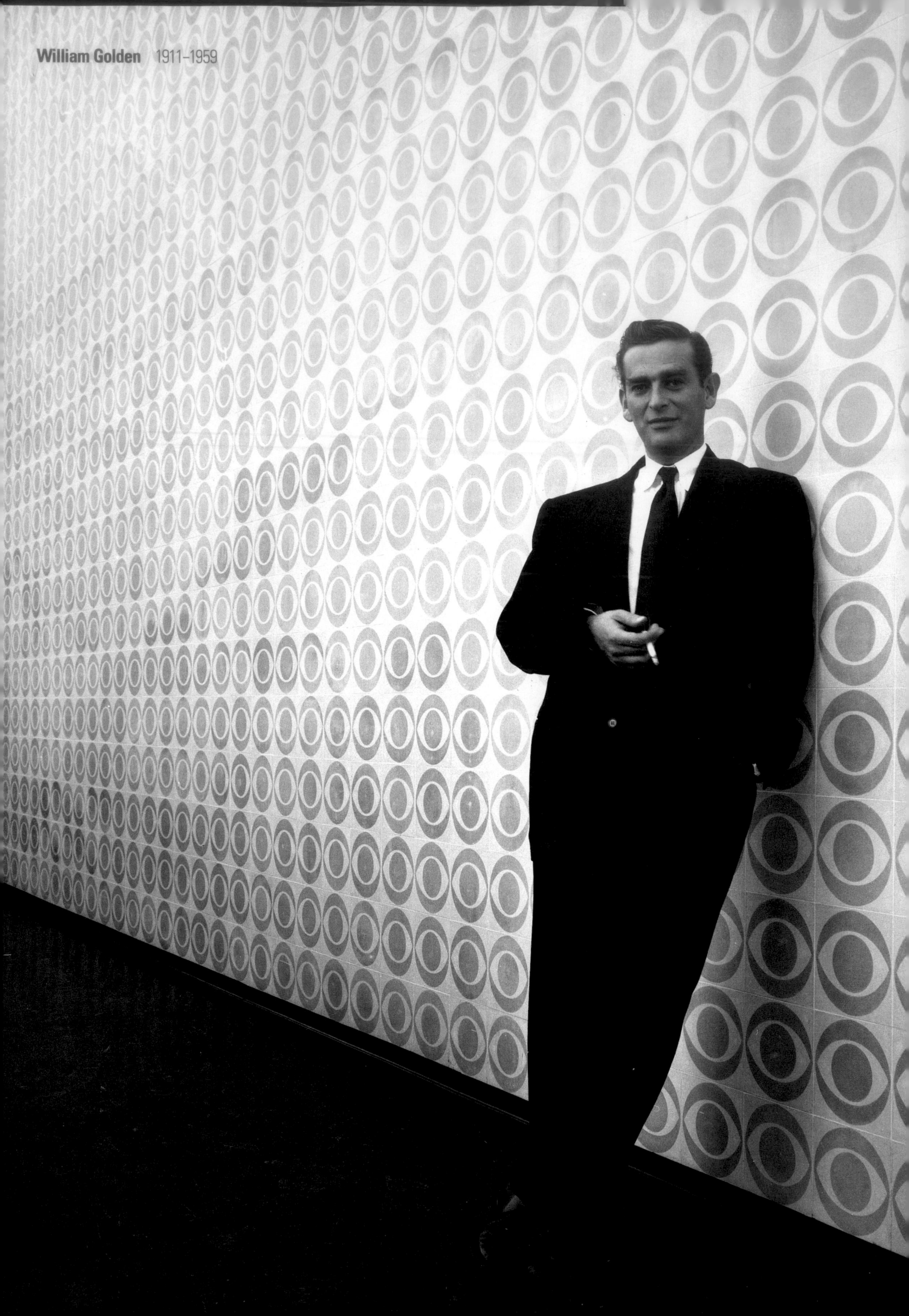

The youngest of twelve children, William Golden was born in lower Manhattan on March 31, 1911, to Aaron Golden, a tailor, and Tobia Entin Golden. His formal schooling ended on his graduation from the Vocational School for Boys, where he took photoengraving and the basics of commercial design. At seventeen, a tough and self-reliant young man, Golden left home to take a job on the other side of the country in a lithography and photoengraving firm in Los Angeles. While there he also worked in the art department of the Los Angeles *Examiner*.

Following his return to New York in the early 1930s, Golden worked as a promotional designer for Hearst's *Journal-American*. Within a few years he had joined the staff of *House and Garden*, one of the Condé Nast magazines. Cipe Pineles, a staff artist at *Vogue* and Golden's future wife (they married in 1942), introduced him to Dr. Mehemed Fehmy Agha, art director of Condé Nast Publications. Agha's early recognition of his talents was the turning point in Golden's career. He learned much during his years of apprenticeship under Agha, who, in Golden's words, "forced the people who worked for him to try constantly to surpass themselves."[1]

Golden left Condé Nast in 1937 to join the promotion department at the Columbia Broadcasting System. He was promoted to art director three years later. Under Golden's guidance the public image of CBS began to match CBS's growing status in broadcasting. When he arrived, the promotion department was small; radio was just coming into its own as a journalistic and entertainment medium (commercial television did not yet exist). Golden created a design program that went beyond promoting CBS as a station: he produced advertising that spoke for the whole medium of radio. Deeply interested in the world political situation, he emphasized radio's ability to bring its audience into touch with historic events. When Vienna fell to Hitler, Golden did a book on it for CBS. He also produced an outstanding book on the fall of Czechoslovakia, as well as a book celebrating the twenty-fifth anniversary of radio, in which he linked radio's history to world events through a progression of news photographs.

In 1941 Golden took a leave of absence from CBS to work for the Office of War Information in Washington. Entering the U.S. Army in 1943 as a private, he served in Europe as art director of army training manuals, and was discharged in 1946 with the rank of captain.

Television and the CBS Corporate Image

When Golden returned to work at CBS after the war, television was the medium of the hour, a medium that enhanced the status of graphic design by promoting visual communication in popular culture. The first stirrings of corporate identity were

in the air. Lester Beall, Paul Rand, Ladislav Sutnar, and other pioneering graphic

designers were developing corporate design programs that often included sym-

bols and logotypes. CBS embarked on its own identity program, of which William

Golden was the chief architect. Through his efforts—backed by a corporate leader-

ship possessed of extraordinary taste and intelligence—CBS achieved a level of

visual elegance that was only much later approached by other companies. Golden

saw his work as a true reflection of what CBS was—and he strove to keep CBS true

to its image throughout his career. "A trademark does not in itself constitute a cor-

porate image," he wrote in 1959. "It is the total impression a company makes in

public through its products, its policies, its actions and its advertising efforts."[2]

The new CBS "house style" was centered around the application of the Didot

Bodoni typeface, which at that time was not available in the United States. Golden

brought it over from France for this project. Staff designers George Lois and Kurt

Weihs became involved in the "Americanization" of the type. Lois recalls, "Bill was

incredible. He took Didot Bodoni, one of the most beautiful typefaces in the world,

blew it up and said to Kurt and me, 'Make it better!' . . . Every CBS Bodoni letter

in the world, Kurt and I redrew. We had to do a letter a week on top of tons of

regular work. We complained but we loved doing it."[3]

The CBS Eye

While the Didot Bodoni was designated as the typeface to be used in all CBS

corporate applications, the famous eye symbol was developed to provide special

identification for CBS Television. Kurt Weihs, who was involved in the project,

remembers that the eye had its beginnings in an article in Alexey Brodovitch's

Portfolio about the then relatively esoteric subject of Shaker design.

Among the illustrations was an eye symbol. Golden picked it up and used it for a
CBS sales portfolio. Then he felt there was more to it and used it for an ad. I redesigned the earlier versions, and it became the mark for CBS Television. We had
done eyes before. Everybody had done eyes; but this one was something that
really worked. I felt the eye could have become the corporate symbol. We saw the
eye as symbolizing CBS "looking at the world."[4]

The eye had its premiere on CBS Television on November 16, 1951, overlaid on a

photograph of the sky filled with clouds.

The symbol was quickly put to use in all aspects of identification for CBS

Television. Its ubiquity caused Golden some second thoughts: "It is used so often

that it sometimes seems like a Frankenstein's monster to me, but I am grateful it is

such a versatile thing that there seems to be no end to the number of ways it can

Copy of an original specimen
showing Didot Bodoni type
brought from France by Golden
and used as the centerpiece of
the new CBS identity program.
The alphabet was extensively
redrawn by Golden's staff to
make it function for the contemporary needs of CBS. It has since
become a popular typeface in
general use in America.

A B C D E

F G H I J

K L M N O

P Q R S T

U V W X Y

Z Æ OE ? !

( ) ; : , . « » - '

1 2 3 4 5

6 7 8 9 0

be used without losing its identity."[5] Years after Golden's death, Lou Dorfsman, his

successor at CBS, offered this praise to the symbol and its creator:

Today as we watch the most transforming medium of our time, there is a Golden
graphic message seen daily by more people than have seen a single mark of modern man. It is that majestically simple CBS eye, as beautifully appropriate when
he designed it in 1951 as it is today. If I can interpret it in the special iconic way of
Bill Golden, it is there to watch over our professional successes as well as spot our
transgressions.[6]

A New Stature for the Designer

For over twenty years Golden worked closely with Frank Stanton, who became

president of CBS. They were friends who shared a drive for excellence and a belief

in the efficacy of good visual form. This was a very productive relationship,

marked by mutual respect. Because design was a matter of high priority for

Stanton, he was willing to give Golden command of the image of the corporation.

As Cipe Pineles put it, "It was [Stanton's] understanding of what a designer could

bring to a company that allowed Bill to develop and go deeply into what the mean-

ing of a broadcasting company is."[7]

Because of his relationship with CBS management, Golden was able to

protect his ideas and his staff and, in large part, have his way with what *he* felt was

the direction for CBS. Though he regularly sent designs to Stanton, it was not for

approval. It was clear that art, design, and advertising were his special areas. His

authority came from his integrity as a designer and his willingness to lay his job on

the line if anyone tried to invade his territory. On one occasion, a layout for a rate

card, submitted to the head of Golden's division, came back by messenger with a

note saying, "I don't like it very much. Let's discuss." Golden's answer was to tape a

drawing pencil to the corner of a large layout pad and send it back with this mes-

sage scribbled across the top sheet: "Let's not! Why don't you make a better one?"

The rate card was produced as originally designed.[8]

Golden carried forward the work Agha and Brodovitch had done in

demonstrating that the designer in a corporation must have a role not only in the

communication of ideas but in the generation of ideas as well. He insisted on play-

ing a part in corporate policy making. Cipe Pineles recalls: "Bill was constantly

urging CBS to spend more money to advertise the shows that gave credit to CBS

as a responsible company—a broadcasting company that revered good theater,

good music, and good news analysis. He realized that he needed to be involved

with administration, because if he wanted to promote the good things he couldn't

just stay in the art department—he had to join the forces which dictated how the

money was to be spent."[9] Golden himself once offered a rather rueful account of what motivates the advertising designer: "Emotionally he is part small businessman and part artist. He isn't strong enough to cut himself off from the world of business to make the personal statement of the artist. He isn't a pure enough businessman to turn his attention completely away from the arts. He somehow wants the best of both worlds."[10] Nevertheless, Golden passed up an offer to become vice-president in charge of advertising and sales promotion at CBS, because he believed it would lead him to become a company man. He preferred, and retained, the title "creative director of advertising and sales promotion."

A Passion for Excellence

CBS Television was clearly in the forefront of graphic design in the early 1950s. The art department, recalls George Lois, was "an atelier; it was the place to be. All the design had to be perfect: the thinking, the concepts, the production. It was the only job in America. . . . Bill protected the place. We did thousands of jobs — ads, trailers, letterheads, charts, and folders. We did tons of work, and every job had to be perfect."[11] A co-worker from those days, John Cowden, remembers "a thousand battles, a thousand scars. But never a negotiated peace for the sake of expediency."[12]

Golden never lost sight of his primary responsibility as a designer: communication of the client's message. We have quoted his description of the advertising designer as "part small businessman and part artist"; on another occasion he asserted that the artist and the designer were "two completely different things."

I think that all the trouble in this field comes from someone's assumption that they are, maybe, the same person. I think the fine artist makes a personal statement about his world, and his reactions to his world. He makes it to a limited audience, or to a big audience — but it's all his. The advertising designer has a completely dif-

"The Egg and I and You," double-page ad that appeared in *Variety* and other trade publications in 1951. Capitalizing on a then-popular film title, Golden used a rebus puzzle to attract attention. Black and white; 16" × 22½".

EDWARD R. MURROW, broadcasting's most respected reporter, brings a new dimension to television reporting today. In his new half-hour program **"SEE IT NOW"** you will see the exciting potential of television as a news gatherer. You will watch a scrupulously edited report of the week's significant events, some of it on film, some of it happening before your eyes. You will meet, face to face, kings and commoners, soldiers and scientists, politicos and plain people who are the masters— or the victims—of events that affect us all. From your own armchair, you will witness the world.

—today at 3:30 on the CBS Television Network **WCBS-TV** *Channel* **2**

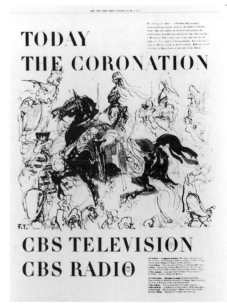

Golden was a friend, colleague, and strong supporter of Edward R. Murrow, whose "See It Now" program became very controversial when Murrow stood up to the red-baiting Senator Joseph McCarthy. This full-page *New York Times* ad with sensitive drawing by René Bouché stood out among its competition in 1951 newspaper pages. 17" × 22¼".

A second full-page *New York Times* ad for Murrow's "See It Now" program has a very different character, with its dramatic photograph by Arnold Newman. 17" × 23".

Full-page newspaper ad for CBS Television and CBS Radio coverage of the coronation of the queen of England in 1953. The ad is composed of a loosely drawn illustration by British artist Felix Topolski and carries the CBS Didot Bodoni for its headline and signature. 17" × 23".

WHICH WAY IN?

How to make the most memorable impression on the human mind is the subject of a now classic debate among the advocates of mass communication media.

It started with the advent of radio and the thesis that the living voice best moved men to action because it could tell your story with human persuasiveness, give it the precise emphasis your message required, and make every line a headline.

The partisans of the printed page have cited arguments as old as Confucius and held that in addition to the authority of the printed word, the use of pictures could arrest, evoke a mood and a desire to buy that the spoken word alone could never achieve.

Since the appearance of television, the debate seems somewhat academic. We'd like to participate in it, but nobody wants to listen. For we've never found anyone who doubted television's impact ... even before it began.

It was obvious at once that television makes the strongest impression. But it was not so certain to make it with comparable economy.

Yet television already wins larger audiences than any other mass medium. And it already reaches more people per dollar than printed media. To deliver the same total circulation today, television costs half as much as a group of magazines and a quarter as much as a group of newspapers.

And in all television, the network with the lowest cost per thousand is CBS Television – 20% lower than the second network.

Advertisers, convinced that the eye and ear work best together, seem to have settled the debate with some finality. In the first quarter of 1954, they made a greater investment in the facilities of CBS Television than in any broadcasting network or national magazine.

CBS TELEVISION

TARGET In 1955 CBS Television achieved a nine-year objective: delivering the most popular programs to the largest audience at the lowest cost in all television.

ferent function. He may be someone who thought he wanted to be a painter—but wasn't. . . . If [the designer is] honest enough, he becomes a professional who can do something special. But this something special is for sale—it is communicating something that is not his own. I think the trouble comes when he tries to make it a work of art, too. I think a lot of designers who are talented and intelligent don't find this very satisfying. But they're not going to find it more satisfying by pretending it's something it isn't.[13]

The maker of good design could, however, have the satisfaction of bringing visual quality to the public and thereby raising the public's expectations of visual quality. The way to attract the public's attention to the client's message, Golden believed, was to be distinguished, subtle, and original. The way to be distinguished, subtle, and original was to avoid the theories and posturing that interfered with clarity of vision. Golden held that clarity of vision was the designer's principal talent, the talent of making a simple order out of many elements. The best design solution, he said, "will look perfectly obvious and inevitable."[14] Of Golden's work, Will Burtin was to say, "There is a mental dexterity and an absolute mastery of subtle details, a complete absence of graphic tricks or intellectual gimmickry, which brings admiration wherever his work appears."[15]

Like Agha, Brodovitch, and Coiner, Golden made enthusiastic use of European ideas in the areas of typography, photography, and layout. Like them, too, he hired European artists and designers themselves. Golden brought the world's top artists in as free lancers to tell the story of broadcasting at CBS in its advertisements and publications.

From artist Ben Shahn (1898–1969) Golden learned a hard lesson—that there are times when one must accept what the artist creates as a foundation upon which to develop the design concept, rather than the other way around. In the early 1940s Shahn was hired to illustrate a war poster. Golden and Shahn met, discussed the project, and decided on an appropriate image. Once Shahn began the project, however, he found himself departing totally from the predetermined image. Though Golden's reaction to the innovation was at first apoplectic—and though he did, in fact, after due consideration reject this particular poster—Golden discovered from this experience "that you get your visual material in hand and look at it. Then you begin to design."[16]

Golden was at his best when he was able to evolve the premise and the concept for the advertising. He was a brilliant copywriter with, as Will Burtin put it, "a sense for the explosive impact of words."[17] Even though Golden was largely self-educated, his mind had scope. "Bill had read enormously and his thinking was clear and bold," recalled Ben Shahn. "The world of advertising and publicity exercised no tyranny over him."[18]

Golden's intelligence was matched by his ability to concentrate on the task at hand. His "infinite capacity for taking pains and attending to detail," wrote John Cowden, "was immediately visible whenever you walked into his office. He had the ability to grasp a complicated problem, strip it down to its bare bones, and then come up with a deceptively simple solution. And he backed this ability with long hours of hard work."[19] Golden's wife, Cipe Pineles, told an interviewer years after his death:

I remember with what pleasure I looked forward to weekends when he brought home type proofs, illustrations, or photographs for a job. Within an hour the room was one mess of papers and photostats, and he was immersed in the business of putting into book form the type, photographs, illustrations and headlines. Making it into a unit became exciting to watch. . . . He had a great interest in making his design readable. It wasn't something he allowed to happen on its own. I would watch him make type tracings until it read right. I kept looking in on him, now and then, saying "There must be an easier way." He would laugh.[20]

And, finally, Golden himself had this to say of the nature of his work: "The kind of effort that goes into graphic expression is essentially lonely and intensive and produces, at its best, a simple logical design. It is sometimes frustrating to find that hardly anyone knows that it is a very complicated job to produce something simple."[21]

With his staff, Golden could be warmly approachable one minute and coolly impersonal the next. This was probably because when he was reviewing an idea, scrutinizing copy, or viewing a layout, the product was more important than the producer. Golden demanded the best from each person, and he required what Judge Learned Hand once called "the intolerable task of thinking." He expected his staff to think for themselves. In this way he forced a great deal of professional development, even though he never taught in a formal way. He would give a designer a job and let him or her run with it. He knew what he wanted to happen, but he trusted the designer to accomplish it. When a designer came to him for a review, he would respond "yes" or "no" without giving a reason. This method, probably learned from his apprenticeship under Agha, was very effective in that it made each designer learn by reasoning out the problem for himself or herself.

As testimony to the sound training Golden provided, at the 1959 New York Art Directors Club Show, thirty-four of the advertisements and promotional mail pieces, including six gold medal winners and Distinctive Merit Award winners,

Ben Shahn was a favorite illustrator of Golden's. "The empty studio," a spread from a four-page folder from 1948, shows a characteristic Shahn line drawing reinforcing the copy message. Black and white; 15" × 23⅜".

Two-page spread from *The Sound of Your Life*, a book that traces the history of CBS Radio by using news photographs. With art direction by William Golden and copy by Robert Strunsky, it was produced in 1950 to celebrate the twenty-fifth anniversary of the beginning of radio. In future years Golden would use the book format to document historic events as part of the promotion of CBS. 8⅜" × 11⅜"

A double-page trade-magazine advertisement for CBS Television, 1955. This ad, which does not use the eye symbol, has a captivating blend of the concept-oriented verbal approach with a textured drawing by Ben Shahn. Like Agha, Brodovitch, and Coiner, William Golden sought out fine artists and photographers for the creation of communications materials. Black, white, green; 12⅞" × 22¾".

herself...
her family...
her world...
her future...

WOMAN!

Announcement folder cover from
1959, with the large CBS Didot
Bodoni type used for the headline, reinforcing the corporate
identity, in this very classical
application with a detail of
Botticelli's Venus. Black and
white; 11″ × 14″.

Double-page *Variety* ad for CBS
Television, 1958. CBS used the
adaptable eye symbol widely in
its early years to make it memorable. Black and white;
14¾″ × 21¾″

UNICEF program announcement,
a full-page newspaper ad from
1956. The playful and literate
illustration, with its allusion to
Gulliver's Travels, was done by
David Stone Martin. 16″ × 18″.

Golden's concern to have CBS
document the news of the time
in its print expressions as well
as on radio and television is evident in this full-page *New York
Times* ad from April 13, 1959. In
addition to the montage of news
photographs, the ad shows the
maturity of the CBS identity,
with both the CBS Didot Bodoni
type and the eye symbol appear-
ing together in the signature.
15⅜″ × 22⅝″.

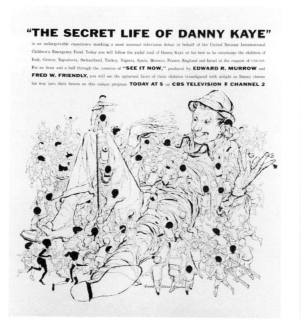

were created by men who had been part of his staff at CBS. Among these were Kurt Weihs, Lou Dorfsman, George Lois, Leonard Sirowitz, Alex Tsao, Norman Greiner, Ray Komai, Rudi Bass, Joe Schindelman, Edward Sorel, Mort Rubenstein, Larry Grossman, and Robert Strunsky.

In developing, directing, and sustaining the visual program at CBS, Golden set an entirely new standard for American design. All the ads, promotional materials, reports, and other corporate design applications done at CBS during his tenure were of a consistently high aesthetic quality. That this level of excellence was taken for granted is especially impressive in view of Golden's insistence that the work was based on business and marketing objectives; in the visual problem-solving process, aesthetics were clearly secondary. It was a case of the corporation's and the designer's objectives being in harmony. As the citation read at Golden's posthumous induction, in 1971, into the New York Art Directors Hall of Fame put it, "If during his tenure William Golden was the perfect art director and tastemaker for this twentieth-century patron, obversely CBS provided the best possible matrix for the crackling, challenging intelligence of William Golden."[22]

Colleagues remember Golden as a quiet man who did not make small talk, who was personally and professionally modest, who was devoted to his job, and who was interested in art, politics, and people. Of Golden's interest in people, Ben Shahn commented that it was not at all of the cocktail-party sort. Instead, he had "a vast compassion for the hurt, the timid, and the beaten-down. Out of this abiding belief and feeling . . . came . . . the basic energy, the motive power of everything that he did."[23]

Golden's very strengths proved, in one important sense, his greatest weaknesses. His drive for excellence and his natural introversion, coupled with habits of smoking and drinking endless cups of coffee, took their toll on his health. He suffered from a painful stomach ulcer from his thirties onward. Because he was not one to complain about his health, certain other ominous symptoms went unmentioned; the heart attack that claimed his life at the age of forty-eight on October 23, 1959, was a stunning shock to his family, his colleagues, and the field of graphic design.

Golden Chronology

1911
Born in New York, New York

1920s
Attends Vocational School for Boys, New York, New York

1928
Moves to Los Angeles to work for a printing firm and in the art department of the Los Angeles *Examiner*

1930s
Returns to New York; works in promotional department at *Journal-American* and then for M. F. Agha at Condé Nast Publications, as member of *House and Garden* staff

1937
Joins Columbia Broadcasting System

1940
Named art director at CBS

1941
Works for Office of War Information, Washington, D.C.

1943–1946
Serves in U.S. Army as art director of army training manuals in Europe

1946
Returns to CBS

1951
Named creative director of advertising and sales promotion for CBS Television Network

1958
Exhibition of his work at Cornell University

1959
Dies in Stony Point, New York

1959
Posthumously named Art Director of the Year by the National Society of Art Directors

1971
Posthumously named one of first members of the New York Art Directors Hall of Fame

1985
Exhibit of his work at Rochester Institute of Technology

Lester Beall 1903–1969

M issouri license plates say "Show Me," and that motto aptly characterized one of Missouri's sons, Lester Beall, who never took anyone's word for anything where design was concerned.

Beall was born in Kansas City on March 14, 1903, to Walter Miles Beall and Effie Thomas Beall. His father, the descendant of one Ninian Beall, a Scotsman who fought Cromwell and ultimately settled in Maryland in the late 1600s, seems to have inherited, and passed on to his son, Ninian's taste for adventure and exploration. An amateur inventor, Walter Beall worked for a printing firm. Effie Beall was an amateur artist who helped develop and direct her son's abilities in drawing and painting. Both parents encouraged Beall to use his hands, and both supported the self-reliance he early displayed.

The Bealls moved from Kansas City to St. Louis when Lester was a small child. When he was seven, the family made its final move, to Chicago, where he stayed until he was thirty-one. His native curiosity about how things worked sparked an early interest in science and engineering, so it was only natural that he should choose Lane Technical School in Chicago when the time came to attend high school. There Beall received practical training in radio, electricity, metalworking, and machining, along with chemistry, physics, and math. The Lane curriculum also included four years of mechanical drawing; this and two courses in life drawing at the University of Chicago would comprise the sum of his formal art training.

On graduating from Lane in 1922, Beall entered the University of Chicago as a physics major. He switched to art history in his junior year and received a bachelor's degree in that field in 1926. He did free-lance work as an undergraduate, producing posters for the YMCA and for the university, and serving as art editor of the yearbook, *Cap and Gown*.

When the University of Chicago offered him a fellowship to pursue a master's degree in art history, on condition that he go into teaching, Beall was torn. His father, who had disapproved of his change of majors from physics to art history, might be appeased by his taking up the respectable position of teacher. On the other hand, he knew himself to be an artist and to need control over his work and his time. Beall made up his mind to follow his own star and began doing free-lance graphic design.

Early Career, 1927–1935

The years Beall spent as a designer in Chicago were a time of tremendous growth for him. Up to 1929 his work was rather conventional; thereafter, a profound change is evident. He discovered the work of the European avant-garde typographers and artists—a discovery that was helped along by his acquaintance with Fred Hauck, an art director at the advertising firm of Batten, Barton, Durstine, and Osborne, whom he met in 1931. Hauck had studied with Hans Hoffman and had visited the Bauhaus. During the two and a half years he and Beall worked together in Chicago, Hauck introduced Beall to the new ideas to which he had been exposed. Perhaps more than anyone else, Beall would be responsible for bringing American graphic design of the 1930s out of its humdrum tastelessness and inaugurating what we now know as effective visual communication.

Free-lance designing depended on clients. Lester Beall was one of the few designers able to balance their egos and creative drives with a sympathetic understanding of clients and their needs. "The essential character and effectiveness of my design," he once said, "—whether complex or simple, feeble or emphatic—is the inevitable product of two points of view, two attitudes toward life, two philosophies: that of the designer/creator and that of the owner/user."[1] Beall's manner was unpretentious. Though essentially reserved and not given to small talk, he projected a readiness for serious discussion whenever the chance arose. Above all, clients could sense the integrity that characterized all phases of his life and work. Once he had established credibility with his clients, it was not difficult for Beall to persuade them to accept progressive visual concepts.

Major Work

Beall moved himself and his design practice to New York in 1935. During his early days there, he worked with two important business clients, advertising representatives Laura Hobson and George Bijur, both of whom allowed him considerable freedom. In his work for Bijur, especially, Beall created strong designs that retain their freshness today. He worked in a number of print advertising campaigns for Bijur, including ads for the Mutual Broadcasting Company in 1939 and an extensive series for *Time* magazine in 1938–1939. The *Time* ads, with their silhouette halftones and dynamic use of angular lines and type, show the influence of avant-garde artists such as El Lissitzky.

From the beginning, Beall ranged freely among the design disciplines— including advertising design, corporate identity programs, product styling, packaging, exhibits, printed literature, murals, annual reports, posters, interior design, and magazines—and worked as a painter as well. When he first moved to New

Cover for a brochure for Heim Jeunes Filles, a high-fashion clothing line offered by Marshall Field, 1930s. Beall used a photogram for an unusual border effect. Black and white, with yellow on dress form; 7″ × 7½″.

Two-page spread from *Photo-Engraving*, no. 3, 1938. This publication, produced by the Sterling Engraving Company in New York, provided designers and graphic artists with technical information about photoengraving and other graphic arts processes. Beall's issues of *Photo-Engraving* show a bold, assertive approach to layout, color, and typography, while maintaining the message's clarity. 8½″ × 10½″.

Cover for the monthly magazine *PM*, November 1937. *PM* called itself "an intimate journal for production managers, art directors, and their associates." Edited by Robert Leslie and Percy Seitlin, *PM* was published by the Composing Room, a progressive type supplier. Through *PM* and the A-D Gallery at the Composing Room, Leslie introduced many young designers to the public. This issue contained an article about Beall written by Charles Coiner, with twenty-one pages of Beall's work. The cover design in its simple arrangement is a fine example of Beall's ability to communicate with a few essential graphic elements. 5⅜″ × 7⅞″.

Spot illustration from 1934 for the Chicago Tribune Travel Bureau. This drawing is one of fifteen reproduced in a limited-edition book by Beall and Fred Hauck in Chicago. Although Beall always loved to draw, his style became much more abstract over the years. 6½″ × 7″.

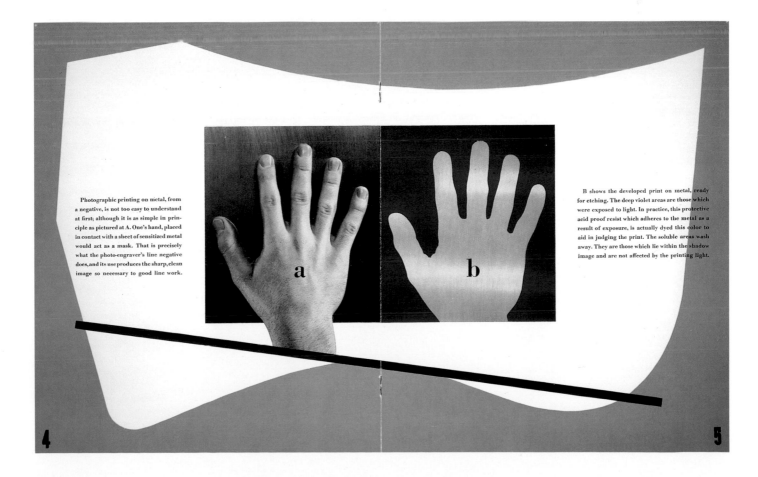

Photographic printing on metal, from a negative, is not too easy to understand at first; although it is as simple in principle as pictured at A. One's hand, placed in contact with a sheet of sensitized metal would act as a mask. That is precisely what the photo-engraver's line negative does, and its use produces the sharp, clean image so necessary to good line work.

a

b

B shows the developed print on metal, ready for etching. The deep violet areas are those which were exposed to light. In practice, this protective acid proof resist which adheres to the metal as a result of exposure, is actually dyed this color to aid in judging the print. The soluble areas wash away. They are those which lie within the shadow image and are not affected by the printing light.

Cover design for *What's New*,
Abbott Laboratories' house
magazine for the American medical profession, February 1941.
The design is reminiscent of such
European avant-garde masters
as Schwitters and Heartfield,
who pioneered the photo montage. 8½″ × 10″.

Experimental photograph by
Lester Beall from the early
1940s. In this image a montage
effect is achieved by placing disparate objects and materials
directly on the model.
10¼″ × 13¼″.

York, an art director told him that "'crashing New York might be a difficult job because you don't draw children, you're not an animal artist, and you don't paint pretty girls—in short, it's hard to classify you. You don't specialize, and art buyers like to pigeonhole every artist.' Naturally, that left me only one alternative—to specialize in nonspecialization."[2] Nonspecialization meant experimentation: "A good designer has to be by nature a student and an experimenter—constantly trying to find new tools for expressing his ideas, as well as new inspiration for the restocking of his creative potential."[3]

Beall helped to change the face of American advertising and graphic design from the 1930s through the 1960s. His work was consistently clear, direct, and communicative. He was one of the early "no frills" graphic designers who emphasized a more functional, information-oriented kind of graphics. William Golden would later remember that, together with Will Burtin, Beall had in the 1930s developed "newer graphic forms and [used] words and images on the printed page to communicate. In their hands these images were employed to make a statement clearer, faster."[4] For Beall, typography had become a machine for communication, just as architecture had become a machine for living.

In March 1944 Beall began to design *Scope* magazine for Upjohn Pharmaceuticals. This series, which continued until 1951, has become one of Beall's best-known efforts and is generally held to be a milestone in editorial design. "Scientists like Beall's treatment of *Scope*," *Interiors* magazine reported in 1951, "because its complicated statistical tabulations, graphs, and data are easy to read and understand; artists study it because it is acknowledged to be one of the most lucid and beautiful examples of layout, typography, and graphic art produced in this country."[5]

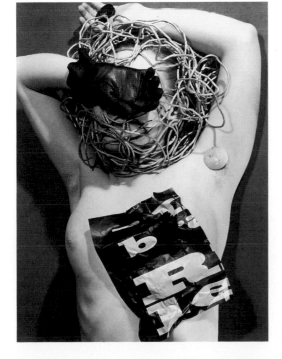

Equally admired was Beall's corporate identity program for the International Paper Company. For this project, which he undertook in 1958, Beall with characteristic thoroughness made a study of the company, its personnel, its facilities, its products. Beall worked hard to establish a unique identity for each of his clients in the midst of what he called "all the vast anonymity." In the interests of his clients, he strove to avoid imitation in design—to refute Frank Lloyd Wright's characterization of most design as "imitation by imitators of imitation." A true expression of the client would necessarily be original, he believed:

A designer . . . has the responsibility to give his audiences not what they think they will want, for this is almost invariably the usual, the accustomed, the obvious and, hence, the unspontaneous. Rather he should provide that quality of thought and intuition which rejects the ineffectual commonplace for effectual originality.[6]

SCOPE

MACHINERY FOR REPAIR

SOLU-B furnishes adequate

amounts of the B vitamins for

the energy releasing

mechanisms in states of stress

SOLU-B® Sterile in 10 cc. vials,
each vial contains, as a
sterile dry powder:
Thiamine Hydrochloride 10 mg.
Riboflavin 10 mg.
Pyridoxine Hydrochloride 5 mg.
Calcium Pantothenate 50 mg.
Nicotinamide 250 mg.
SOLU-B, 5X®, Sterile in 30 cc. vials,
each vial contains, as a
sterile dry powder:
Thiamine Hydrochloride 50 mg.
Riboflavin 50 mg.
Pyridoxine Hydrochloride 25 mg.
Calcium Pantothenate 250 mg.
Nicotinamide 1260 mg.

"TRADEMARK, REG. U.S. PAT. OFF."

SCOPE VOL. 11 No. 7, MARCH 1948, PUBLISHED BY THE UPJOHN COMPANY, KALAMAZOO, MICHIGAN

Full-page ad from *Scope*, May 1949. Color; 9″ × 11¼″.

Cover for "A Guide to Lester Beall," catalog for an exhibition of Beall's work at the A-D Gallery, 19 November 1945. The juxtaposition of elements, the use of negative space and antique imagery, all show Beall's understanding of the visual syntax of progressive European art movements. Color; 5⅜″ × 7⅞″.

Page from *Scope*, May 1949, accompanying an article about red blood cells. Beall's ability to transform complex information and processes into a simple, understandable message is evident here. Color; 9″ × 11¼″.

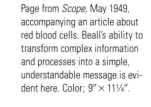

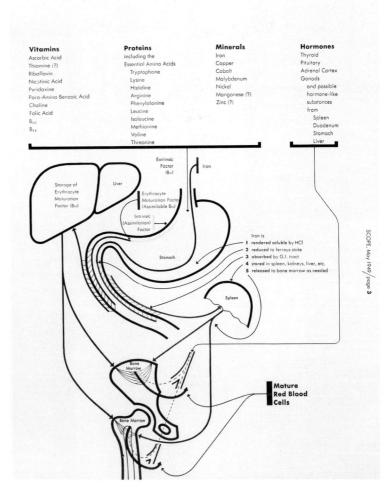

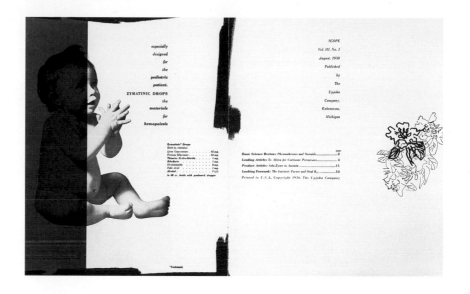

In order to accomplish this, the designer must effectively sell "his attitude of constant and intuitive experimentation as opposed to allowing himself to be 'researched' into and out of all the so-called answers."[7]

Research must be done, however, and the designer must devise methods for doing it that deserve the client's confidence. "The truly aware designer," Beall said, "is ever concerned with structuring his own individualistic data system, and if his system is an effective one, he can presume to impose answers upon his client, simply because he knows he is qualified to do so."[8]

Beall's project for the International Paper Company may well be his best-recognized corporate identity program; he produced many memorable symbols and programs, however, for such prestigious firms as Rohm and Haas, Merrill Lynch, Caterpillar, Connecticut General, Martin Marietta, The New York Hilton, and Emhart. Beall was one of the very first designers involved in developing comprehensive visual identity programs for corporations.

Beall was as effective designing in three dimensions as he was in two. He began to do package design in 1936, and by 1957 fully half of his work was in this area. His packaging solutions for Wiss Products were notable for readable type, strong, simple shapes, clear colors, and easy, foolproof opening construction. The Pond cosmetics packaging dramatically increased that line's sales and made it a best-seller in its price class. In spite of these pragmatic concerns, however, Beall remained a visual formalist. *Gebrauchsgraphik* magazine, as early as 1939, showed examples of his work and commented that it "is anything but the cleverly solved results of a lifeless and bold constructivism, simply because the artist's creativity is everywhere sufficiently visible and finds its natural expression

Cover for *ORS*, a Davis and Geck house organ for operating-room staff, 1950s. Another application of the photogram of a flower ensemble with flat overlayed color bands and typography. 6″ × 9″.

Cover for April 1951 *Diameter*, a literary arts magazine. The format was standard for each issue, with only color changes in the ellipses. The free brush script gives an informal tone to the publication. 6″ × 9″.

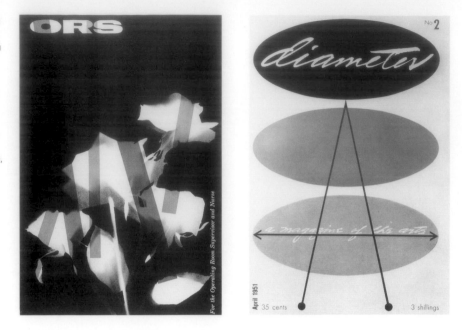

Identity mark for the International Paper Company. One of Beall's best-known and most effective works, this mark is timeless and ranks with the CBS eye symbol as a classic in visual identity design.

in an astonishing use of formal elements. His work reveals a perfect command of the typographical medium and an unerring feeling for the proper arrangement of surfaces."[9]

For Beall "the way a man lives is essential to the work he produces. The two cannot be separated."[10] In 1952 he opened a design office at Dumbarton Farm, his home in rural Connecticut; here he exercised careful oversight on each project and was able to foster and maintain a closely knit staff. Beall was committed to a "people-oriented" approach to design, because he defined design as "integral to life—ultimately bound up with the lives of people. And the near-perfect answer is to be found in a personal and group integrity."[11] The New York office was closed in 1955, and all work thereafter done at Dumbarton Farm. Lester Beall died in New York City on June 21, 1969, after a long illness. He was sixty-six.

What Makes Good Design?

There is no real distinction between art and design, Lester Beall contended; the only true distinction is between things well and badly done. Throughout his own career as a designer, Beall continued to work as an artist and participated in numerous exhibitions of painting and drawing. "Art in any form is a projected emotion using visual tools," he once said.[12] The same gifts and training that make any successful practitioner of the visual arts will make a successful designer—except that the designer must gain in addition a sound knowledge of the principles and techniques of business communication. To his "intuitive approach to his work" must be added "the cold logic that must successfully reach out to people."[13]

Spread from Lester Beall Inc. promotional publication showing packaging designed in 1960 for the International Paper Company. A well-designed corporate identity program is one that allows the elements (logo, color, typography, format) to be adapted to all the applications of the company. Each page 8½″ × 8″.

Spread from International Paper Company publication showing additional applications of the corporate identity elements that Beall designed. Each page 8½″ × 8″.

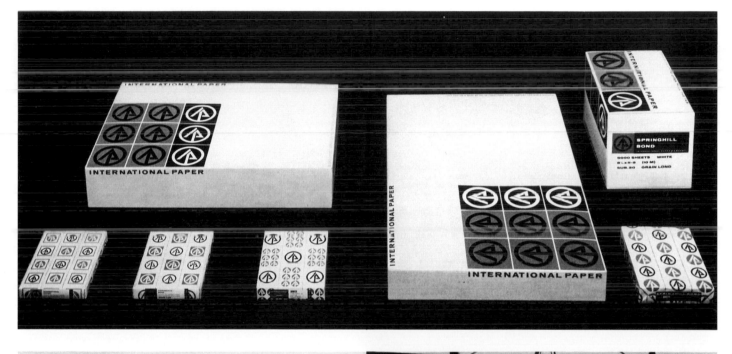

Front and back covers of portfolio "Communication" for the International Paper Company, 1961. Dorothy Beall collaborated with her husband on the research and writing for this project. The purpose of the piece was to promote International Paper's business papers through a deluxe showing of printing and sample letterhead designs. Color; 11¼" × 11¼".

Spread from "Communication" for International Paper Company, showing historical series of communications artifacts. Color; each page 11" × 11".

Identity mark for Merrill Lynch, Pierce, Fenner, and Smith, 1961. Beall's stated goal for this project was to "create an emphatic corporate symbol, and its precise application to all working materials."

Identity mark for Titeflex Inc., a producer of flexible metal tubing. In designing this mark in 1958, Beall made the letterform "T" conform to an acute curve, thus suggesting the product of the firm.

Motion test of identity mark for the New York Hilton Hotel, created in 1961. Photograph shows how a well-designed mark maintains legibility even when in motion or out of focus.

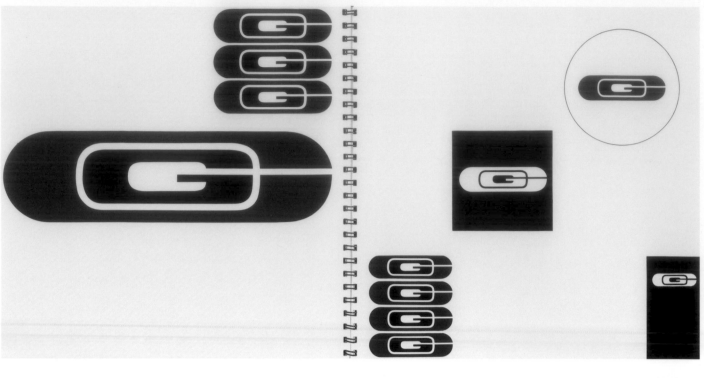

This spread from the Connecticut
General style book shows different versions of the distinctive
''CG'' symbol designed by Beall
in 1958. Each page 9″ × 9″.

Beall was an early proponent of corporate identity. These spreads from the Connecticut General style book show typographic standards in the program and the eighteen colors Beall selected for secondary use in printed literature.

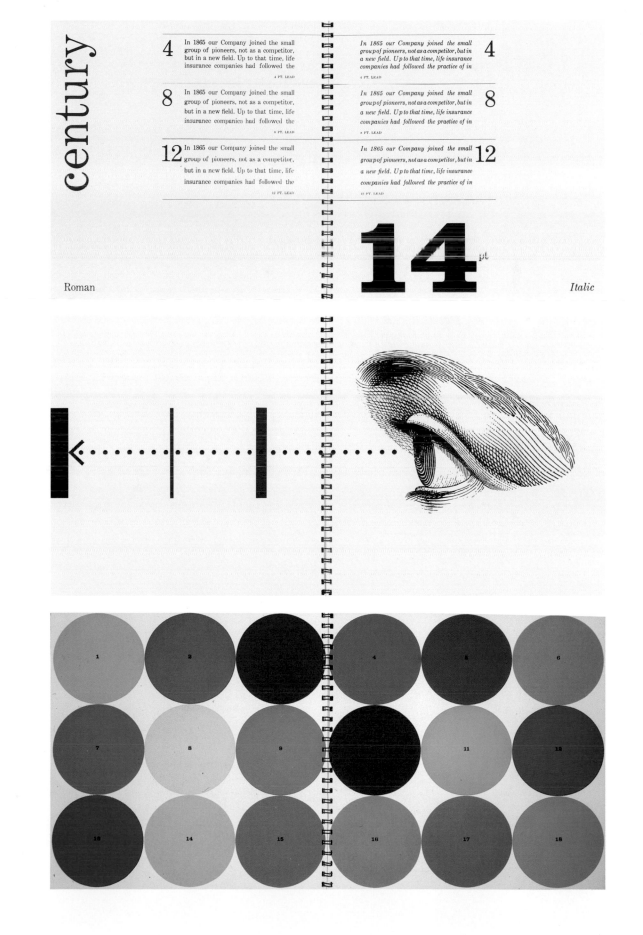

In an article written for *Print* magazine in 1958, Beall celebrated the new-found authority of the designer in the commercial world:

Creativity, which is the basis of all communication in its original form or forms, is, in the eyes of more and more segments of business management, identified with the designer. . . . Today's designer stirs and keeps alive the creative aspects of any and all types of business, and, assuredly, no business, whether it be the advertising business or the business of making shoes, can afford to be without him, for the designer has proved time and time again that good design is good business.[14]

Along with the freedom of expression that his respected status conferred, the designer bore a serious responsibility:

— a responsibility that embraces the fact that applied good taste is a mark of good citizenship. Ugliness is a form of anarchy that should be stamped out wherever it is evident, for the anarchy that ugly cities, ugly advertising, and ugly homes breed, can never be separated from the individual. Ugly lives produce bad citizens, and bad citizens can eventually part us all from the freedom of expression that the concept of individuality strives to maintain. . . . The most effective prevention of public and official cynicism must come from our own quickened sense of moral obligation to strive for an ever-increasing elevation of our tastes and an appreciation for the dignity and the future of our culture.[15]

The word "integrity" appears often in the writings and recorded remarks of Lester Beall. To him it always meant both personal honesty and aesthetic soundness: two indivisible qualities.

One microcosm of the threat of a visually poor environment is the detrimental characteristic prevailing in the philosophy of advertising and public relations that has indubitably cemented sales records to the product, regardless of the intrinsic worth of the product. In other words, such philosophies, in a razor-edged competitive market, lack a rudimentary sense of the meaning of integrity. The result in part is the manufacturer who produces products of expediency; and the craftsman (the labor community) who demands more and more monies without equally important demands for products with structural aesthetic honesty.[16]

He decried the tendency among artists and designers toward a competitive aggressiveness manifested by the desire for quick money and prevalence on the "marquee." The proponents of this posture are, too often, the museums, galleries, art schools, magazines and others with eulogies of what are the foremost trends. Hence, the so-called "fine artists," as well as graphic designers, must share some concern in perverting and being perverted by these instruments of fashion-setting trends with an attendant drift away from the integrity of expression.[17]

The purpose of art, said Aristotle, is not to represent the outward appearance of things but, rather, to represent their inward significance. Lester Beall knew the truth of this statement. The solution of every design problem, he knew, lies intrinsically within the subject; it takes a designer equipped with both sound training and intuition, capable of hard thinking and hard work, to enact that solution.

Beall Chronology

1903
Born in Kansas City, Missouri

1922
Graduates from Lane Technical School, Chicago

1926
Bachelor of Philosophy degree, University of Chicago

1927–1935
Free-lance designer in Chicago

1935–1955
Design office in New York

1937
One-man exhibit of design at Museum of Modern Art, New York

1937
Issue of *PM* magazine features Beall's work

1938–1940
Redesigns twenty magazines for McGraw-Hill

1944–1952
Designs for Upjohn Company

1945
One-man exhibit at A-D Gallery, New York

1948
One-man exhibit at Society of Illustrators, New York

1952
Opens design office at Dumbarton Farm, Brookfield, Connecticut; also maintains New York office, until 1955

1953–1961
Designs for Torrington Manufacturing Company

1954–1969
Designs for Martin Marietta

1955–1964
Designs for Connecticut General Life Insurance Company

1958
Designs corporate identity program for International Paper Company

1959
Participates in Typography-U.S.A. forum in New York

1959 1969
Designs for Caterpillar

1960–1968
Designs for Merrill Lynch, Pierce, Fenner, and Smith

1961
Designs corporate identity program for the New York Hilton

1962
One-man exhibit at American Institute of Graphic Arts, New York

1964–1969
Designs for Rohm and Haas Company

1969
Dies in New York, New York

1972
Inducted into New York Art Directors Club Hall of Fame

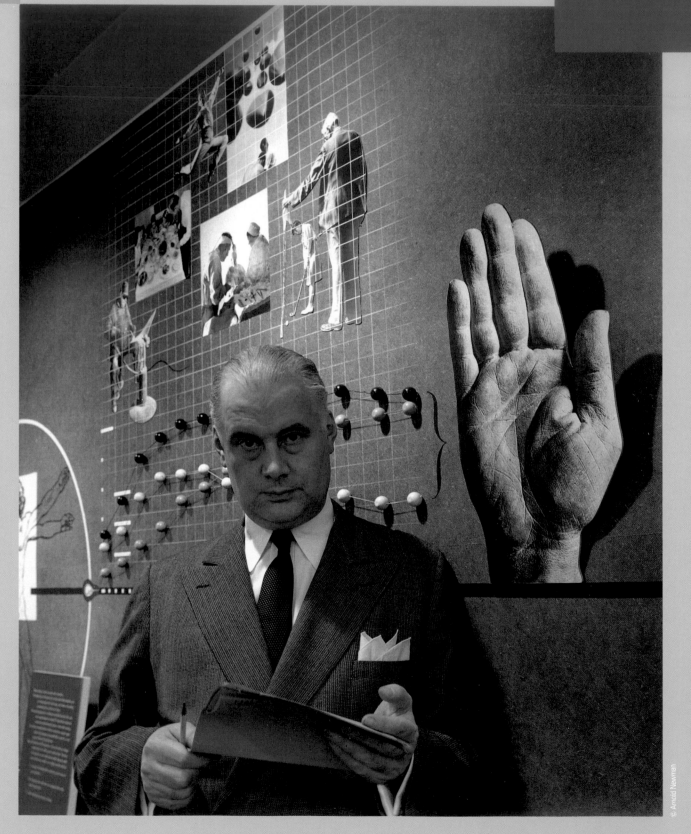

Will Burtin

W ill Burtin, son of August and Gertrud Burtin, was born in Cologne, Germany. His father was a French chemist of Flemish lineage. Between the ages of fourteen and seventeen, the boy was apprenticed to a typesetting shop in Cologne. The director of the shop perceived Burtin's aptitude and saw to it that he was enrolled in evening graphic design classes at the Cologne Werkschule, where he later taught from 1927 to 1930, after completing his own studies.

Burtin opened an exhibition design studio in Cologne in 1927. He was soon attracting clients from all over Europe. In 1932 he married, and took on as partner in his studio, Hilda Munk (1910–1960), who had been a fellow student at the Werkschule.

The young Burtin opposed Victorian typography and rejected its tradition, because he felt it imposed too much of a limitation on visual problem solving. "Setting type according to the rules of Didot, Bodoni, and the Jugendstil seemed to be the highest accomplishment when I became a typesetter in Germany," he later wrote. "However, it gradually appeared to others and myself that those princi ples applied to the symmetry of classical book titles and book work and ignored the fact that the kinds of communication had expanded and changed."[1] Burtin's goal was to express a new content and effect quick understanding. He felt that this goal could be achieved through the new typography then being developed in Europe, which involved using sans serif typefaces and asymmetric layout. He was deeply influenced by Cubist, Constructivist, Dada, and Suprematist art, as well as by the new architecture, photography, and technology of the 1930s.

With the Nazi ascent to power, Burtin, as one of Germany's leading designers, was invited to become the "house" designer for Hitler. In 1938 he was requested to contribute his skills to the design of the Berlin World's Fair. Burtin felt no sympathy for the Hitler regime, and his wife's family was Jewish. Late in 1938, when it became clear that he would not otherwise be able to avoid working for the Nazi party, he and his wife fled Germany. Setting off ostensibly for a Mediterranean cruise, they ended up in the United States, where they were sponsored by relatives of Hilda's who lived just outside Washington, D.C.

The Burtins settled in New York City. Already known to the American design community, Will Burtin was quickly invited to show his work at Robert Leslie's Composing Room. (Leslie, a physician-cum-printer, and Sol Cantor, a linotype technician, had opened the Composing Room and its exhibition gallery—the first gallery in the United States devoted to the graphic arts—in 1921. Here, through a series of exhibitions of the work of European and American type designers, art directors, illustrators, commercial designers, and academic designers, they worked

to educate the community at large about the role of design in contemporary soci-

ety.) Through the show Burtin met and formed friendships with William Golden

and his wife, Cipe Pineles, and with other designers working in New York.

Burtin applied himself without delay to the task of learning to speak, read,

and write English. He was soon engaged in free-lance design work and in teaching.

In 1939 he joined the faculty at the Pratt Institute, where he remained for decades,

becoming chairman of the Department of Visual Communication in 1959. During

the 1950s he also lectured at the Parsons School of Design.

There was a close connection between Burtin's personal drive for knowl-

edge, his propensity for teaching, and his own design career. Carol Burtin Fripp, his

daughter (now a television producer in Toronto), has commented, "I think that he

thought that all of his career was a form of teaching; that all of it was supposed to

Will Burtin teaching at Pratt Institute, 1942. Students of that period recall that even though Burtin's use of English was limited, he was a very effective teacher.

convey ideas; that design was the powerful medium to convey those ideas."[2]

Regretting his lack of formal schooling, Burtin engaged in an intense, lifelong pro-

cess of self-education. In his opening address as president of the 1955 International

Design Conference in Aspen, Colorado, Burtin remarked, "Thomas Jefferson said

once that education is a process in which we learn how to learn. . . . To learn how to

keep learning is the mark of a civilized man." The designer, he believed, had an

obligation to become well informed in a wide range of fields of knowledge, if his

work was to fulfill adequately its task of "general cultural improvement."[3]

Burtin's Work: Performance in the Service of Ideas

In 1939, just months after his arrival in the United States, Burtin was commis-

sioned to design a major exhibition for the United States pavilion at the World's Fair

in New York. In 1943, during World War II, he was again involved in major work for

design decade

Color cover for special insert to February-March 1942 issue of *A-D* on the work of Will Burtin between 1930 and 1940. 5½" × 8½". Published by the Composing Room in New York under the editorial guidance of Dr. Robert Leslie, *A-D* was the successor to Leslie's earlier publication, *PM*. Both magazines were important communications vehicles for the graphic arts industry in the 1930s and 1940s. Through them and through Leslie's A-D Gallery, new talent in graphic design was introduced to the market.

Cover for *Vesalius*, a booklet probably produced by Upjohn in the late 1930s. This design was included in the 1942 issue of *A-D* that showcased Burtin's work from the 1930s. Here a modern, abstract line image is combined with a classical typographic element. Orange and black.

A spread from the 1942 *A-D* insert on Burtin, showing his Christmas card for *Fortune* magazine, printed on celluloid, 1942. Color.

VESALIUS

Booklet cover

Advertisement for Fortune

Burtin has successfully adapted his technique for printed advertising to problems in three-dimensional, educational displays.

A characteristic example of this work was the exhibit of the Federal Works Agency at the New York World's Fair, 1940, which explained to the public the achievements of the Government's program. Part of this exhibit (see page 18) was designed for easy transport.

15

Christmas card for Fortune

22

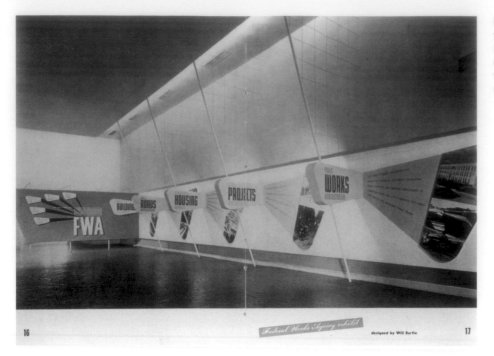

Federal Works Agency Exhibit at
the New York World's Fair, 1940.
Designed for easy transport, this
display explained to the public
the achievements of the government program.

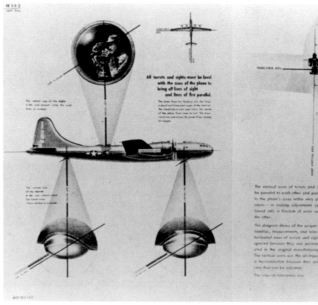

Cover and spread for *Gunnery in
the A-26,* a manual for the U.S.
Air Force published in November
1944. The two-page layout
shows Burtin's use of diagrams
to teach complex processes in a
simple way.

the government, this time in the design of training manuals for the U.S. Air Force. These publications were intended to make aerial gunners out of teenaged boys. The visuals were extremely complex: the gunner had to learn about the gun's mechanisms and operation in battle, and he had to learn methods for judging the correct angle and duration of firing, depending on the speed and direction of motion of each of the planes involved. Burtin was committed to the safety of the gunner, who "was engaged in a serious business in which his life might depend on the swift functioning of his knowledge and equipment. He deserved dignified treatment and the clearest possible statement of facts."[4] These manuals are a superb example of Burtin's ability to make complex information understandable. Burtin was assisted in this project by two important colleagues, Lawrence Lessing and Max Gschwind, the latter an extraordinary designer of charts and diagrams.

Fortune

In 1945 Burtin became art director of *Fortune* magazine, a position he held until 1949. The typographical expertise, the skill in integrating text and image, and the gift for making complexity intelligible that he had honed in the course of his government work all served Burtin well in his new sphere. Ladislav Sutnar in his book *Visual Design in Action* characterized Burtin's innovations at *Fortune* in this way:

In the second half of the nineteen forties *Fortune* magazine spearheaded the exploitation of new visual techniques for maps, graphs, and charts. Examples from this period show two basic approaches. The first may be called "purist." Charts and diagrams were compressed into a two-dimensional projection. Color was used only to facilitate a better understanding. . . . The second way might be called a "dramatized" approach. In this technique a new dimension is added. Typical of this is the grouping of map segments on a poster-like cover.[5]

In addition to his technical experience, Burtin brought a sophisticated aesthetic and psychological sensibility, as well as good taste, to his work for *Fortune*. He employed the finest designers and photographers of the day, including Lester Beall, Gyorgy Kepes, Arthur Lidov, and Walker Evans. Burtin's own layouts for "The Physician and the Bomb" in the May 1946 issue exemplify his efforts to integrate text and illustrative material.

Upjohn

During the years at *Fortune* Burtin was, as his colleague there, George Klauber, recalls, "preoccupied with the graphic communication of scientific phenomena and theory; and the models and illustrations which he conceived were modest preludes to the magnificent work to follow for Upjohn Company."[6] Burtin's

Cover from *Fortune Magazine*, June 1946, with illustration by Arthur Lidov. Burtin's influence is evident in this piece with the diagrammatic illustration highlighting the issue's theme of fundamental science.

1948 exhibition at the Composing Room, "Integration: The New Discipline in

Design," demonstrated his desire to clarify scientific information rather than to

allow it to remain a puzzle. While at *Fortune*, he maintained free-lance accounts,

including the Upjohn Company, a large pharmaceutical firm with headquarters in

Kalamazoo, Michigan. When Burtin left *Fortune* to open his New York studio in

1949, Upjohn became a major client. Upjohn had an enlightened management

who were open to Burtin's ideas. Near the end of Burtin's tenure at *Fortune*, he

and George Klauber collaborated on a comprehensive program involving

Upjohn's logo, printed matter, advertising, films, packaging, exhibitions, and even

new plant architecture. Burtin became Upjohn's general consultant and art direc-

tor for its house publication, *Scope.* Burtin and Upjohn were a perfect match, and

the relationship continued for more than twenty years, until 1971. Burtin's

graphics for Upjohn are remembered for their simplicity and directness, with

emphasis on the message.

Full-color advertisement for the Upjohn Company's vitamins, 1948–1949. For this ad, Burtin asked his young daughter, Carol, to do the handwriting for the copy. 10¾" × 13⅛".

With *Scope* Burtin continued a tradition of distinguished graphic design

begun by Lester Beall. The magazine, whose audience was largely physicians,

existed to improve the understanding of modern therapeutics and to enhance

Upjohn's sales of pharmaceutical products. To both its articles and its advertising

Burtin gave a coherence of presentation that arose from his own thorough grasp

of the subject matter, gained through painstaking research that required as much

of his time as the art work. The *Scope* issues from these years are classic exam-

ples of Burtin's ability to create functional design with unique beauty.

In 1958 Burtin completed one of the major projects of his mature years, the

Cell Exhibit for Upjohn. He referred to his model of a human blood cell as an

"exhibit sculpture"; it used the language of technology and science to generate a

greater sense of the beauty inherent in the environment. In the research stage for

this project, Burtin studied medical literature and interviewed physicians,

biologists, molecular chemists, and geneticists. "Every doctor and scientist,"

recalls George Klauber, his assistant on the project, "had a different interpretation

of what the cell structure would look like enlarged one million times. There was

absolutely no agreement, so Will, with characteristic audacity and insight, made

the decisions necessary to complete a working model. The result was an over-

whelming success—although a few of the very men who could never take a

stand or commit themselves, were quick to challenge it."[7]

The model was 24 feet in diameter. Viewers could walk into and around the

cell, experiencing its contours and its component parts from all points of view.

Cover for *Scope*, winter 1955.
8¾″ × 11″.

Cover for Burtin's first issue of
Scope, 1948, a magazine for the
Upjohn Company. Burtin's work
for *Scope* shows his gift for pre-
senting technical information in
a clear and understandable way.
Burtin was able to bring taste
and beauty to otherwise ordinary subject matter. 8¾″ × 11″.

The Upjohn Cell Exhibit. The observer could walk into and around the cell.

Burtin's daughter, Carol, stands in front of an element in the center of the Upjohn Cell Exhibit, 1958. Photograph by Ezra Stoller, Burtin's colleague and friend.

Will Burtin flanked by *(left)* Professor Michael Swann, science consultant, and *(right)* Gordon Taylor, script writer, for the BBC television program that made use of Burtin's cell model during its stay in England in 1959. Photograph copyright BBC.

Detail of the Brain Exhibit, 1960, showing structure and the thousands of lights that would indicate thought paths. Photograph by Ezra Stoller.

The Upjohn Brain Exhibit, 1960. This display was a precursor of the light show or multimedia event. The audience was presented with a dazzling display of images and color as the process of a thought was illustrated.

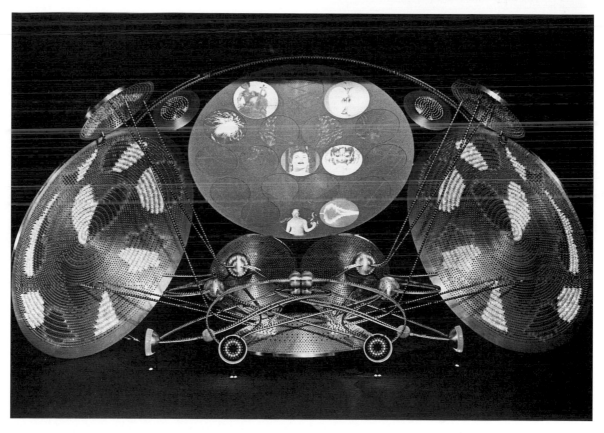

The exhibit captivated thousands of people in the United States and in England, where it was moved in 1959 for a special BBC program on biology. After that, until its materials disintegrated, it was at the Museum of Science and Industry in Chicago. The cell model was later used in textbooks and articles in popular magazines around the world.

The Cell Exhibit generated other similar projects for Upjohn, notably one demonstrating the processes of the human brain. Burtin defined the design problem as a search for an audiovisual mode of demonstrating the sequence by which the main product of the brain, a thought, evolves. He consulted with structural engineers, physicians, physicists, chemists, and other specialists in order to ensure accuracy in the presentation while preserving simplicity and clarity of communication. At an early stage of development it became obvious that to be understandable, the form of the exhibit should not be based on the anatomy of the organ but rather on the thinking process itself. The model focused on the interactions of the dominant brain sensations, sight and hearing. Burtin was tempted to integrate the remaining three senses of taste, smell, and touch, but his research persuaded him that their inclusion would introduce an unmanageable degree of complexity.

The Brain Exhibit, completed in 1960, was a precursor of what was to become popular as the "light show" or multimedia event. Through projected image, sequence, lights, and color—among the components of the exhibit were 45,000 lights and 40 miles of wire—Burtin conveyed the workings of the mind in a way never approached before.

"In retrospect, the most profound experience of working on 'The Brain,'" Burtin wrote in 1964, "was the idea that the problem of how we think about thinking had become a design problem as well. In tracing the logic by which awareness of reality and dream is established, I felt often as if I were looking into the reasoning of creation itself."[8] Attendance at the New York staging of the Brain Exhibit was so heavy that Upjohn considered the fabrication of a second unit for Europe. For months it was the biggest nighttime attraction on Park Avenue.

In 1964 Burtin, Roy Tillotson, Dr. A. Garrard MacLeod (Upjohn's director of special projects), and Bruce MacKenzie produced a booklet for Upjohn entitled *The Visual Aspects of Science*, which makes a strong case for the visual beauty in the world of science. The layout and design of the booklet are examples of Burtin's precision in form and content, emphasizing the message.

Burtin's work for the Upjohn Company ended in 1971 owing to changes in corporate leadership and accompanying budget cutbacks. The new management assumed that the company could successfully move ahead on the momentum of Burtin's previous work.

Eastman Kodak

A "total design" challenge faced Burtin when he was asked to design the Eastman Kodak Exhibit for the New York World's Fair in 1964. Burtin attempted what he called "a totally integrated communications environment in which every aspect of the architecture and all visual devices are part of one coherent story plan which has scope as wide as life itself and as intimate as the first openings of a baby's eyes."[9] Burtin's idea was to arrange the photography exhibits fluidly throughout a free-form pavilion surrounding a tower of rear-projected, constantly changing images. His pavilion resembles the architecture of Eero Saarinen, most particularly the TWA Terminal of 1956–1962 at New York's Kennedy Airport. Burtin conceived the roof line as giving the impression of a floating magic carpet.

Model for the Eastman Kodak Building at the New York World's Fair, 1964. Photography exhibits were arranged fluidly in a free-form pavilion that surrounded a tower of rear-projected, changing images.

Industrial Design magazine reported about the project, "It manifests a new turn in today's architecture. The project is an effort to conceive space appropriate to contemporary human needs, form, and materials. This structure may alarm and frighten a few, but to eyes sore from rectangular wastelands, it may provide relief."[10]

Other Projects

From 1949 to 1970 Burtin's office was busy with other clients besides Upjohn and Eastman Kodak. Work was done for IBM, the Smithsonian Institution, Mead Paper, Union Carbide, Herman Miller Furniture, and the United States Information Agency. The University Circle Development Foundation of Cleveland, Ohio, asked

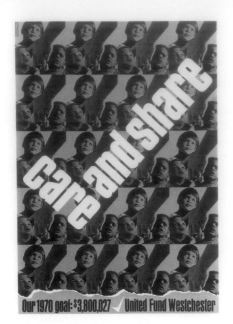

Color poster for the United Fund
of Westchester County, New
York, 1970. 16⅝" × 24¼".

Burtin in 1968 to do a study of integrated street signage and lighting. With his usual thoroughness, Burtin made a systematic photographic study of the characteristics of the entire University Circle neighborhood. Then he selected a three-block section for a closer study. From the research emerged a design proposal that included a pole-grid sign system, bus shelters, maps, parking booths, interior signs, and a manual for project implementation.

Philip Meggs reminds us that for Will Burtin, "man . . . is the most important consideration of a designer. . . . The individual's 'emotional, physical, and intellectual response' and understanding of the information communicated should be the yardstick used to measure or evaluate a visual communications design."[11] In Burtin's work priority is consistently given to the clear communication of ideas. He strove to teach, and he included among the learners those who normally are not at ease with the terminology and complex information of science.

Burtin's wife Hilda died in 1960. The following year he married the designer Cipe Pineles, widow of William Golden. Burtin continued his active design practice almost up to the time of his death, of cancer, in New York City on January 18, 1972.

Design as an Environment for Education

In a 1971 article Burtin asserted, "Modern graphic presentation is a form of visual reasoning whose purpose is to heighten and clarify man's understanding of the modern world."[12] For Burtin, art and science were one. Visual communication must be based on four "realities": the reality of man, as measure and measurer; the reality of light, color, and texture; the reality of space, motion, and time; and the reality of science. Science, Burtin believed, "allows people to see the workings of nature, makes transparent the solid and gives structure to the invisible."[13]

An exhibition of Burtin's work at the Composing Room in 1948 had as its theme "Integration: The New Discipline in Design." The exhibition was a synthesis of Burtin's approach to design as a mirror of the changing social and technological scene. "It was here for the first time," George Klauber writes, "that a designer, utilizing all the graphic and structural tools at his disposal, presented his philosophy of design as a living document and environment for education."[14]

Burtin felt that his major strength was an ability to reduce problems to their basic components. Only by discovering the essential, underlying structure of a complex phenomenon, he believed, could one impart harmony and unity to its

Foldout cover for *Defense of Life*, monograph designed for the Upjohn Company in 1969. Burtin's goal in this project was, he said, "to make a graphic introduction to the vast and complex topic of the entire inflammatory process." Color; 8⁷⁄₁₆" × 11".

Color cover for program booklet used at the Vision 65 conference at Carbondale, Illinois, 1965. 9¾" × 9¾". This world congress on new challenges to human communications was organized by Burtin and is remembered as one of the finest design meetings ever convened.

Color poster for Burtin's second conference, Vision 67: Survival and Growth, held at New York University in 1967. 18" × 18".

representation. George Klauber remembers being "captivated by Will's exuberant ability to espouse, tackle, ponder, and produce a solution to many problems that at the outset seemed insoluble. And it always seemed inevitable and appropriate." He continues:

The excitement of working with Will was engendered by this process of design analysis and synthesis. It was so stimulating that in its evolution "the moment of truth" was as emotionally charged as great theater, and often I would feel tears of fulfillment well up within me. Burtin and I worked best together after everybody had gone home for the day and the phone had stopped ringing—that is, anywhere between 5 p.m. and midnight and not infrequently on weekends.[15]

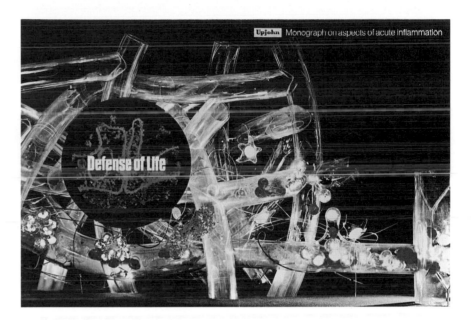

Burtin's daughter recalls that her father "worked all the time. First he went after the overall concept. He didn't do it in bits and pieces. He had to get the goal first. I remember his attention to detail in every area of his life. Those were basic parts of his craft as well. He lived his life the same way. He was very gentle and always working, a constantly listening person." She sums up his operating principles as these four: "simplify, communicate, teach, and learn."[16]

In 1956 Burtin moved his office into the studio occupied until his untimely death by Alvin Lustig. "It was a very serious place," recalls Burton Kramer, the eminent Canadian designer and a former Burtin employee. "I worked with Yves Zimmerman and Betti Haft. Other interesting people like Roman Vishniac and Andy Warhol were in and out all the time."[17] Moving into Lustig's fashionable studio was a new departure for Burtin and his staff, although Klauber remembers that "little changed in working relationships except that they had room to expand. The 42nd Street office in New York was devoid of any pretensions, as Will had little interest in a jazzy working space."[18] Burtin was neat in his habits, and the entire office reflected his meticulousness. He felt that clutter was one of

the deadly sins. The office did, however, contain artifacts from scientific projects: prototype propellers, medical charts, pieces of plastic once used for exhibit models. A caring and considerate boss, Burtin nevertheless valued the work they were engaged in above all else. Betti Broadwater Haft, a staff member in the fifties, recalls, "Burtin ran the office like a teacher: problem given, critique, and then back to the board."[19]

Burtin was often the focus for bringing together designers in public forums. He organized and was a speaker at numerous conferences, including the International Design Conference in Aspen in 1955, the Typography-U.S.A. Conference in 1959, the Vision 65 conference at Southern Illinois University (sponsored by the International Center for the Typographic Arts), and the Vision 67 conference in New York. Burton Kramer recollects that he tended to speak "over the heads of the people, since he was interested in things beyond the pedestrian level."[20]

In speeches and in his extensive writings about design, Burtin stressed the social responsibilities of the designer. The ultimate purpose of all design endeavors, he reminded his colleagues, is improving "the quality of our human environment."[21] In an article entitled "The Means and Ends of Package Designing," he wrote, "The advances in the segments of merchandising research and technology will not constitute progress unless they are matched by an equally tenacious endeavor to improve the standards of taste. . . . Considering the moral values which the pursuit of beauty can give to daily life, it is absolutely necessary that we fight against the argument that taste or beauty is optional in . . . design."[22]

Burtin had come to grips with the hard reality that most Americans have their aesthetic sensibilities shaped by the sheer volume of graphic, packaging, and industrial design that surrounds them from the moment the alarm goes off in the morning to the moment the book or magazine is closed or the television is turned off at the end of the day. "To regard a grocery shelf as an art gallery would be absurd," he wrote, "but it would nevertheless be a good principle to think of . . . design not only as a promotional means but also as a demonstration that inventiveness and good taste, while fulfilling all the requirements of commerce, can help to produce an aesthetically pleasing environment for living people."[23]

Burtin Chronology

1908
Born in Cologne, Germany

1922–1925
Apprentice in typesetting shop, Cologne

1927–1930
Teacher at Cologne Werkschule

1927
Opens exhibition design studio, Cologne

1938
Emigrates to the United States

1939
Begins teaching at Pratt Institute

1943–1944
Designs gunnery manuals for U.S. Air Force; designer for Office of Strategic Services

1945–1949
Art director at *Fortune* magazine

1948
Exhibit at Composing Room in New York

1948–1971
Design consultant for Upjohn Company

1949
Opens studio in New York

1958
Designs Cell Exhibit for Upjohn Company

1960
Designs Brain Exhibit for Upjohn Company

1964
Designs Eastman Kodak Exhibit at New York World's Fair

1971
Medal from American Institute of Graphic Arts

1972
Dies in New York

lustig

Alvin Lustig 1915–1955

"Design is a form of justice between men and material. If this moral tone is offensive to some, remember that design is concerned with relationships and relationships are always good or bad, never neutral."[1] A characteristic pronouncement by Alvin Lustig, whose short life was a quest for both aesthetic and spiritual order—two names, he held, for the same thing.

Lustig's pursuit of harmony was never merely on his own behalf. Complementing the speculative and the philosophical in his temperament was a strong belief that he needed to bring others, be they clients or design students, to share his vision of using design to reshape the world. Despite the gaps in his own formal training and the brevity of his career, Lustig influenced the course of design and design education in ways that continue to be felt today.

In believing that the fine arts must not be divorced from the applied, that design must enhance and use technology rather than fight against it, and that the artist must use his gifts in the service of society, Lustig was, of course, a product of his time. He grew up in Depression-era America, where Roosevelt's New Deal WPA was providing jobs for artists, among them Ben Shahn, who recorded national events like the trial of Sacco and Vanzetti in painting and who documented photographically the poverty of farmers for the Farm Security Administration. Social Realist muralists—Thomas Hart Benton, Diego Rivera, Jean Charlot— depicted American life, ways, and ideals on the walls of public buildings. During this period, Frank Lloyd Wright was evolving, largely through domestic architecture, his ideas about design for a democracy. Finally, the designers, painters, and architects fleeing fascism and war in Europe in the 1930s and early 1940s—among them Gropius, Bayer, Moholy-Nagy, and Brodovitch—brought with them an array of formal visual ideas that refreshed and excited young American designers. Of particular influence on graphic designers were the Europeans' ordering of space and design elements and their use of photomontage, large letterforms and symbolism, asymmetric balance, and contrasting type and pictorial matter.

If Lustig's milieu did much to shape his social consciousness and his aesthetic values, the intensity and single-mindedness with which he applied them were all his own. Born a Jew, he became a Christian for a period in his life and assumed the task of helping to initiate a rebirth of Christianity. When asked by a friend how he could reconcile his life's project of reviving Christianity with typographic design, Lustig replied that religion and design were simply parts of the same whole.

Early Years

Lustig was born on February 8, 1915, in Denver, Colorado, to Harry and Jeannette Lustig. Five years later the family moved to Los Angeles, California, where Harry Lustig had accepted a job as head salesman for Metro Pictures. Alvin attended Los Angeles High School and, as a hobby, developed his skills as a magician. By the time he was sixteen he had been admitted to membership in the American Society of Magicians and the International Brotherhood of Magicians. Putting on magic shows became a regular event, and he soon became interested in doing posters to advertise his performances. During his senior year in high school, Lustig's art appreciation teacher, Aimee Bourdieu, showed him the posters of E. McKnight Kauffer and A. M. Cassandre, which, according to Lustig, transformed his way of seeing.

Business paper for Interstate Management Corporation, done in California in the late 1930s. Lustig used elements from the printer's typecase in designing the "IM" logo. His use of capital letters with wide letterspacing is characteristic of the period. Brown lettering on gray and darker gray paper; 8½" × 5½".

In 1933 Lustig entered Los Angeles Junior College, where he spent one year. At the same time he served as art director for *Westways*, a periodical of the Automobile Club of Southern California. At the junior college he took Richard Hoffman's printing courses and art courses from Harry Kablick. The year 1934 saw him enrolled in the Art Center School in Los Angeles for the one year of professional art courses he would experience in his career.

At this point Lustig became particularly interested in architecture. He introduced himself to Richard Neutra, a young architect whose contemporary style impressed him. Then in 1935 he departed for Wisconsin to study with Frank Lloyd Wright at Taliesin East. Characteristically, Lustig had sought out a master from whom he could study both design and architecture, a master outside the mainstream of education.

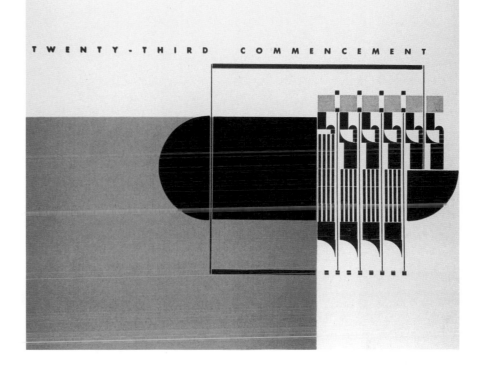

Cover for Los Angeles High
School's 23rd commencement
folder. In the late 1930s Lustig
contributed designs for his high
school's events. This one is composed of geometric shapes and
lines from the typecase. Black
and brown; 8½" × 8¼".

Self-promotion piece in two
colors plus metallic gold, late
1930s. Other designers and
typographers had used the
elements of the typecase to
create images; Lustig, however
combined the designs with
impeccably clean typography for
a distinctive and unique style.
Lustig saw this kind of design as
"attractive to those who, with
limited budgets, seek fine design
and typography." 10¾" × 8".

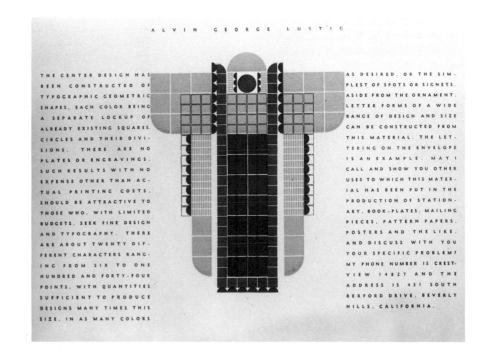

The exposure to Wright at Taliesin was short-lived. He was soon chafing under the strictures of doing things the Wright way. An anecdote from his Taliesin visit has him being shown into a room and instructed to wait there for Wright. As he glanced around, Lustig noticed that there was a blue vase against a blue wall and a white vase against a white wall. He exchanged the blue vase and the white vase. Wright entered the room, and as he spoke his first words to young Lustig, replaced the blue vase against the blue wall and the white vase against the white wall.

Lustig next sought instruction from Jean Charlot, the Mexican fresco artist, who had been working and teaching in the United States since 1929. The period of independent study with Charlot in Los Angeles in 1936 marked the end of his formal and informal education.

Work

Between 1937 and 1943 Lustig designed books for the Ward Ritchie Press in Los Angeles. "Alvin had made for himself an attractive small studio from a formerly dull room he had rented in a building on West Seventh Street," recalls Ward Ritchie. "He had built himself a desk with a few drawers in which he kept a few fonts of sans serif type and an assortment of rules and geometrical ornaments with which he would create amazing designs."[2] Much of Lustig's work throughout his career involved type alone. His knowledge of painters and painting led him to apply to his design the "new" concepts of space that had given vitality to modern art. Philip Johnson has commented about Lustig that "there was focused into his person a channeling from the great modern painting of Picasso, Matisse,

The versatile Lustig was a popular interior designer in Los Angeles and New York. This color photograph, taken in his own office in Los Angeles in 1947 or 1948, shows his use of bright colors juxtaposed with natural wood finishes in geometric arrangements.

Lustig worked with architect Victor Gruen in designing the signage for the Northland Shopping Center near Detroit in 1952. This was a pioneering collaboration between the architect and the graphic designer.

and Mondrian. He focused their teaching into the creation of public symbols which make our surroundings."[3]

Soon after establishing himself at his West Seventh Street studio, Lustig had to move. Ward Ritchie explains: "Alvin's artistry was his undoing. When his landlord saw how he had transformed the murky back room into such a handsome studio, he decided that the rent was too low and doubled it, which was more than Alvin was willing to pay. He mentioned his dilemma to me and I offered him space in our printing shop, rent free." On his arrival Lustig completely redesigned Ritchie's shop, making it "functional, forthright, and attractive."[4]

In 1939 Lustig began doing book and jacket design for the New Directions publishing firm in New York. New Directions remained a major client of his throughout the 1940s and 1950s, and at various times during these years Lustig lived and worked in New York. In 1948 he married Elaine Firstenberg, who was to become his amanuensis when blindness made him unable to carry out his design ideas.

Lustig refused to specialize. To him all design was a matter of form and color, and the differences between projects were largely technical. Lustig was among the first practicing designers to see the role of the designer as that of a synthesizer. Besides books and book jackets, his own wide-ranging career included work on magazines, letterheads, catalogs, advertising, record albums, signage, furniture, fabrics, interior design, letterform design, symbols, trademarks, identity programs, sculpture, architecture, and even a one-man helicopter. His work with Victor Gruen in 1950 on the signage for the Northland Shopping Center in Detroit was the first example of direct collaboration between a designer and an architect.

For Lustig, design was largely something that one did in one's head. The internal, cerebral quality of his methodology is touched on in his whimsical self-characterization: "I make solutions that nobody wants to problems that don't exist." When he went blind in 1954 (a complication of the diabetes of which he died the next year), he kept working by conceptualizing solutions and dictating directions to his wife, Elaine. So keen was this skill that Lustig could specify color for a graphic design by making references to a portion of a famous painting.

His sketches were small, brief annotations grouped on a large pad, showing mental processes that might have been going on for days. James Laughlin, publisher of New Directions Books in the forties and fifties, commented that the

Cover for *Fortune* magazine,
December 1946. Lustig's use of
color often reflects his formative
years in California. This design
makes use of both photographic
and flat graphic elements.
10¼″ × 13″.

Lustig was an accomplished
fabric designer, as seen in this
piece for LaVerne Originals, done
in 1946–1947. The fabric was
bright red with a black pattern of
linear motifs superimposed.

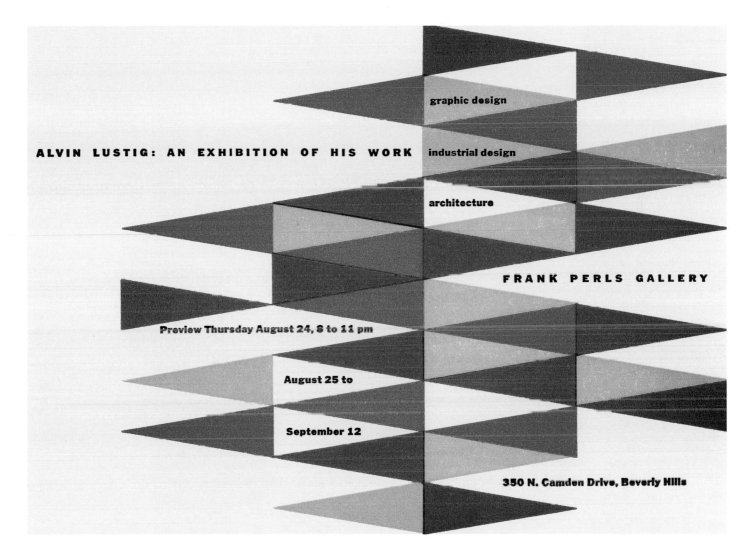

ALVIN LUSTIG: AN EXHIBITION OF HIS WORK

graphic design

industrial design

architecture

FRANK PERLS GALLERY

Preview Thursday August 24, 8 to 11 pm

August 25 to

September 12

350 N. Camden Drive, Beverly Hills

Invitation/announcement card for "Alvin Lustig: An Exhibition of His Work," held at the Frank Perls Gallery in Beverly Hills, California, in 1949. Lustig believed graphic designers should exhibit their work in galleries: he made little distinction between the fine and the applied arts. 7" × 5".

HISTORY
AS THE STORY OF
LIBERTY
BENEDETTO CROCE

MERIDIAN BOOKS   published by The Noonday Press
Sewn-bound for durability   M 17 $1.35

Jacket design for *History as the Story of Liberty*, by Benedetto Croce, 1954, for Arthur Cohen's Noonday Press. Color; 4¼″ × 7¼″.

Page of pencil sketches for paperback jacket design for Knut Hamsun's *Growth of the Soil*, 1950. Lustig would make small thumbnail sketches such as these for most projects. 11″ × 14″.

forms Lustig used were shaped in his mind—a mind that seemed as inexhaustible as Picasso's or Klee's. Lustig belonged to the small body of designers who are incapable of distinguishing between form and content, because they know them as one and the same. His was the realm of forms, symbols, and images.

Lustig's approach to design evidenced a kind of order and harmonics that had old roots. Some have called it an extension of the "intellectual approach" of the Bauhaus. Tschichold's title page from *The Printer's Union Textbook* was a very strong influence in his development; he considered it one of the most beautiful pages in modern typography. His graphics also owe much to the tradition of the 1930s as exemplified by Cassandre and Kauffer.

With clients, Lustig was tenacious in pursuing his own vision. Arthur A. Cohen, president of the Noonday Press in the early fifties, remembered that when Lustig was hired to provide advice on Noonday's paperback covers, he attempted to redesign the whole publishing firm. Lustig felt that he was most effective when working with clients who were capable of clearing their minds of preconceptions about the way the product should look. Ideally, the client should even take the initiative in embarking on a process of understanding the meaning of design and its skills.

His advice to a client was to remember that the designer's relationship to a problem "should be a comprehensive one and not fragmentary. He is an expert in the control of physical elements, and if [he is] allowed to work out the problem in his own terms, the result will be an effective piece of printed persuasion."[5]

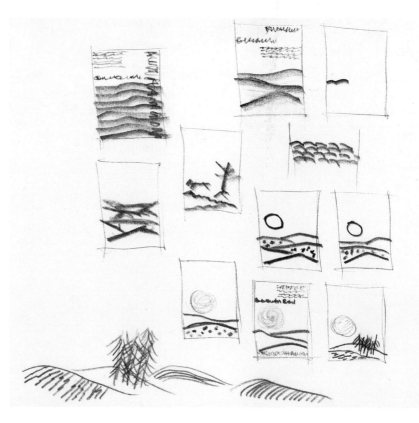

Book jacket design for *Amerika*, by Franz Kafka, late 1940s. This jacket combines hand-drawn line with a bold geometric star treatment. Color; 5″ × 7¼″.

Jacket for the novel *The Final Hours*, by José Suárez Carreño. Lustig was a major force in designing the modern paperback and hardcover book jacket. This cover, with its cross composition, has the stable yet dynamic quality characteristic of Lustig's work. Color; 5½″ × 8¼″.

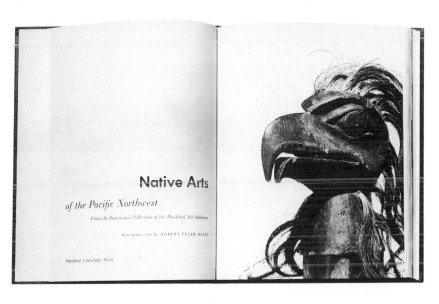

Title spread for *Native Arts of the Pacific Northwest*, Stanford University Press, 1947. This book design was one of Lustig's finest; he masterfully blended types with bold asymmetric layouts of the Indian artifacts. Black and white; 9″ × 11¼″.

Lustig was convinced that the public for his design was, by and large, "form blind." He saw the "redesign" of the client as the first responsibility of the designer. To accomplish this goal, he devoted a great deal of time to talking with his clients—and he did not always listen to what they had to offer to the dialogue. In enforcing his own design criteria, this sophisticated, elegant, courtly man could be demanding, self-centered, and almost obsessive. "Purity of heart is to will one thing," said Kierkegaard. Alvin Lustig surely willed one thing: an order and harmony of design that was connected to the finest art traditions of the past.

Teaching

From the mid-1940s on, while he continued to run a design office, Lustig increasingly devoted his energies to education. Although he had essentially designed his own educational experience himself, he believed in the possibility of a truly effective design school. He had, he said, "a naive faith that somehow school is the area in which a kind of experimentation and research, not possible in the workaday world, is taking place."[6] Indeed, of the practicing designers of the thirties, forties, and fifties, Lustig was the one with the greatest appreciation for what might be done in art education.

Frequently education seems to fragment the art experience for the purpose of systematic study. The division of the fine from the applied arts is a major line of fragmentation, and it is one of the things Lustig had struggled against in his own education. A central concept of Lustig's was the synthesis of the fine and applied arts rather than their separation. His work as a design curriculum consultant in the early 1950s bears out his strong belief in synthesis—of the visual arts with real life, of the fine with the applied arts, and of design with technology. "The great cultures of the past," Lustig said, "had neither the concept of 'art for art's sake' nor 'art for use's sake.' Somehow the tradition grew in such a way that the artist found himself, and yet had room for experiment. He was part of the total developing tradition. This is probably the greatest challenge that will face us now and for the next hundred years."[7]

Lustig's first teaching experience was at the Summer Art Institute at Black Mountain College, North Carolina, in 1945. There he met Josef Albers, who recommended him in 1951 as a consultant to the University of Georgia, to help develop its design program, and later asked him to help establish the design program at Yale. The latter project was probably the most far-reaching of

In 1949 Lustig had a one-man exhibition of his work at the A-D Gallery in New York. For this presentation he designed a special installation structure to hold the panels of work. This photograph shows sections of the exhibit with book jackets, ads, structural design, and his one-man Roteron helicopter.

Scale model for the exhibit at the A-D Gallery. Lustig made the stands in graduated sizes so that they would fit in one box, and designed panels and connectors that attached them to one another.

Detail of a drawing that shows the construction of the A-D Gallery exhibit. The exhibit traveled later to the Walker Art Center in Minneapolis and the Frank Perls Gallery in Beverly Hills.

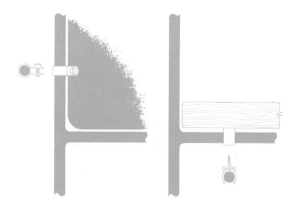

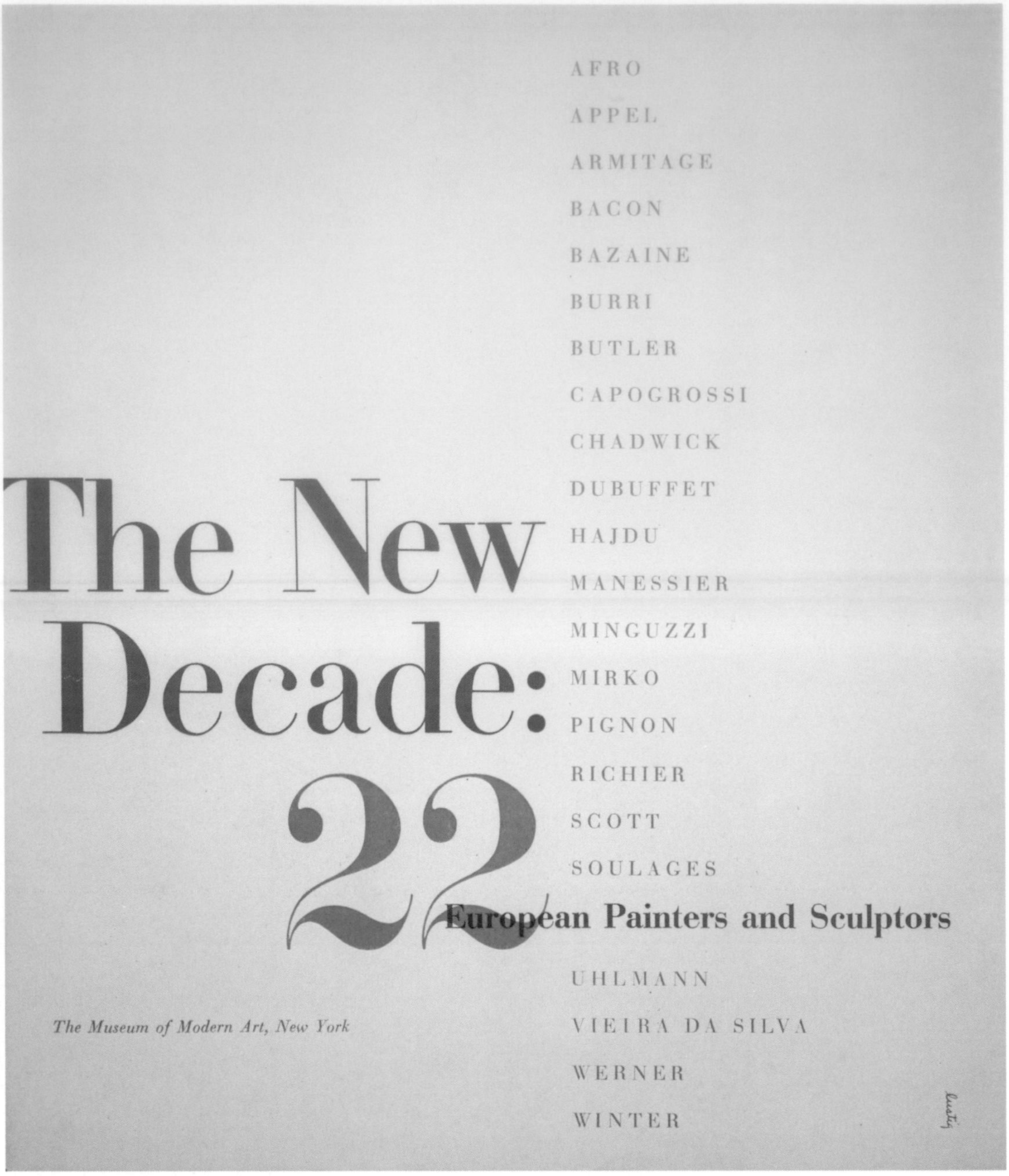

AFRO
APPEL
ARMITAGE
BACON
BAZAINE
BURRI
BUTLER
CAPOGROSSI
CHADWICK
DUBUFFET
HAJDU
MANESSIER
MINGUZZI
MIRKO
PIGNON
RICHIER
SCOTT
SOULAGES

The New Decade:
22
European Painters and Sculptors

The Museum of Modern Art, New York

UHLMANN
VIEIRA DA SILVA
WERNER
WINTER

Catalog cover for the Museum of Modern Art's "The New Decade" show of twenty-two European painters and sculptors, 1954. This piece is another example of Lustig's love for designing with typography alone. 8½" × 9¾".

Magazine advertisement for the Container Corporation of America's "Great Ideas of Western Man" series. The quote from John Ruskin concerns the benefits of education. Lustig uses a simple box format, with color for emphasis and many typestyles to suggest diversity and to reinforce the verbal message. 8½" × 11".

Letterhead in black from Lustig's New York office. A classic piece of Lustig design, it shows the clear influence of Tschichold and the idea that typography was often adequate in itself for a satisfactory solution to a problem. 7¼" × 10½".

ALVIN LUSTIG

graphic design 1936-1955

March 1 to March 25, 1977

Opening: Tuesday, March 1 at 5:30 p.m.

Exhibition planned by Elaine Lustig Cohen & Tamar Cohen

The American Institute of Graphic Arts

1059 Third Avenue, New York 10021

Invitation card for posthumous
exhibit of Lustig's work at the
American Institute of Graphic
Arts, March 1977.

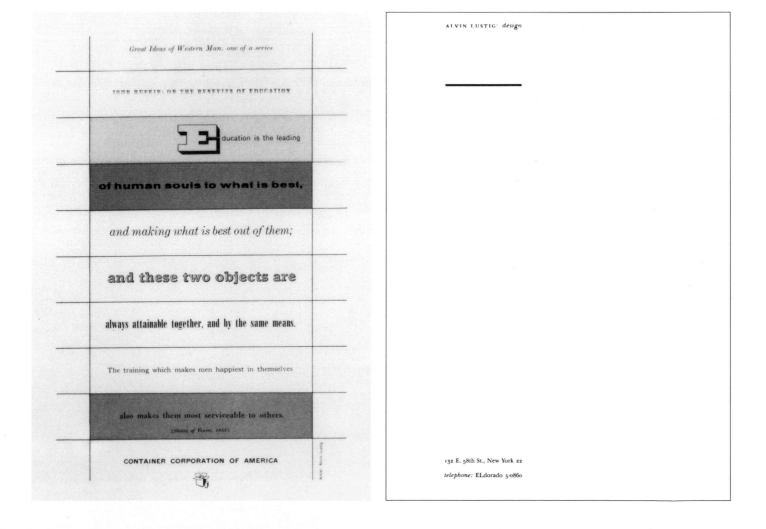

Lustig's educational involvements. The Yale program crystallized his belief that design needed to be related to the fine arts and to the social system. The best design program, he felt, was one closely related to a painting program. In addition, it must bridge the gap between the ideal of art school and the reality of the working designer—must "produce people who are capable of finding some reasonable specialized activity that will give them a 'hook' onto the existing economic situation and at the same time, produce people who have the vision and moral integrity to continue to be creative people even though they are involved in a technical society."[8] Good design, Lustig knew, is design related to and springing from its time. If a designer "lacks the inherent ability, the insight, the intuitive selection of what is right for his time," he wrote, "he will not go far and will eventually be forced to enter another field. If he is equipped with these characteristics, he will lead the way to new and more effective approaches to design in all its forms."[9]

Though reticent in most of his dealings with people, as a teacher Lustig was entertaining and eloquent. Lou Danziger, a student of Lustig's at the California Art Center in 1947,[10] remembers his teacher as having "the most incredible mind. It was most inspiring. He was a teacher who never talked about design, but he made you feel that design was the most important thing that you could do, and everyone just killed themselves for him."[11] His ability to inspire students to excel showed itself at Yale too. Alvin Eisenman, of Yale's Graphic Design Department, remembers going past the design classroom after midnight the night before Lustig's once-a-week class met, and seeing all the lights burning. Lustig's students would bring in multiple solutions to a problem, hoping that he would approve of one. He was a patient teacher, who never raised his voice or lost his temper. Instead, when things were not under control, he simply remained quiet and walked away. According to Arthur Cohen, publisher and Lustig's longtime friend, Lustig could locate where a person's mind was and would undertake its reprogramming, using his expressive eyes and hands to make his points clear.

When he knew that he would soon be blind, Lustig invited his major clients to a cocktail party at which he explained the situation to them. By late 1954 he had completely lost his sight. He continued to teach and to supervise design projects, with the help of his wife, until his death on December 5, 1955. In his short lifespan he had accomplished much, had conceived and given the first expression to many of the ideas and strategies we take for granted today.

Lustig Chronology

1915

Born in Denver, Colorado

1920

Family moves to Los Angeles, California

1933

Attends Los Angeles Junior College; art director of *Westways* magazine

1934

Attends Art Center School, Los Angeles

1935

Studies with Frank Lloyd Wright at Taliesin, Wisconsin, for three months

1936

Independent study with Jean Charlot

1937–1943

Designs and prints at small print shop in Brentwood, Los Angeles; designs books for Ward Ritchie Press

1939

Designs book jackets for New Directions Books, New York (1940s through 1950s)

1944–1946

Visual research director for *Look* magazine, New York; teaches at Black Mountain College, North Carolina

1946–1950

Free-lance design practice in Los Angeles; designs several shops and apartment houses; teaches at Art Center School

1949

Exhibition at the A-D Gallery, New York; exhibit travels to the Walker Art Center, Minneapolis

1950–1955

Design office in New York; visiting critic in design at Yale University; designs signage for Northland Shopping Center in Detroit, in collaboration with Victor Gruen

1953

Exhibition at Museum of Modern Art, New York

1955

Dies in New York

Ladislav Sutnar 1897–1976

L adislav Sutnar was one of the scores of European artists to whom the United States offered a haven before and during World War II, and who richly repaid their adopted country with their skills and knowledge. Sutnar was born to Vaclav and Rozalie Cyclerova Sutnar on November 9, 1897, in the city of Pilsen, in what was then Bohemia (a part of the Austro-Hungarian Monarchy) and is now Czechoslovakia.

Sutnar's education in art consisted of the study of painting at the Prague Academy of Industrial Art and at Charles University and the Technical University, also in Prague. In 1923, at age twenty-six, he became a professor of design at the State School of Graphic Arts in Prague, in addition to maintaining his own design practice; in 1932 he was named director of the school. Sutnar taught himself constructive and functional typography; commercial and industrial advertising; poster, magazine, and book design; industrial design; and exhibition design. In the early 1920s he visited the Bauhaus and became an ardent advocate of its functional approach; by the early 1930s he was known as the originator of modern design in Czechoslovakia.

Forming a Design Methodology

When Ladislav Sutnar arrived in America in 1939, his evolution as a graphic designer was complete. He had absorbed the ideals of the Bauhaus: he believed that design should apply to every dimension of life and that every design problem must be approached on its own terms with as unbiased, fresh, and flexible an attitude as possible. He had embraced the teaching of the Constructivists that every design solution must have a logical structure, as opposed to being spontaneously improvised or influenced by personal feeling. And he was a proponent of Tschichold's "new typography," with its asymmetry, its use of white space and contrast in general, its use of heavy rules and bars to demarcate information units, its simplification of letterforms, its use of heavy initial letters to enhance the communication of the message, and its preference for photography, machine-set type, and the primary colors. These and other schools had merged during the 1920s into an international movement that sought, in Sutnar's words, "to define the fundamental principle that a language of form should be used only as a means to express function in design."[1] The function of graphic design was to communicate ideas and information as efficiently as possible. Simplicity, order, and precision must therefore characterize every graphic presentation.

Sutnar believed that the designer, as problem solver, ought to be capable of working in many fields of design. Early in his career he acted on this belief by

This textbook cover from 1931 is an early classic Sutnar design. It echoes solutions of the Bauhaus, Bayer, "the new typography," and the Russian Constructivists. Sutnar was a prominent designer and teacher in Czechoslovakia during this period and has been compared to Gropius in the design leadership he exerted in his homeland.

Sutnar designed this theater playbill in 1934 for the New Theater, Prague. The content is articulated by simple geometric means into a series of parts. It is easy to read whether in a dark theater interior or on a street corner. The heavy black bar at the top left becomes an identity element for the poster.

Magazine cover designed by Sutnar in 1929, when he was working in Czechoslovakia. This avant-garde design with the large negative space and asymmetric organization shows the influence of the Bauhaus and Jan Tschichold. This and a number of the other Sutnar examples are from his *Visual Design in Action*, 1961, where most appear in black and white. The dimensions and, with some exceptions, the colors of the original works could not be determined.

Sutnar was an accomplished exhibit designer. This photograph of the famous Brno exhibit of 1929 shows his functional approach applied to a three-dimensional problem.

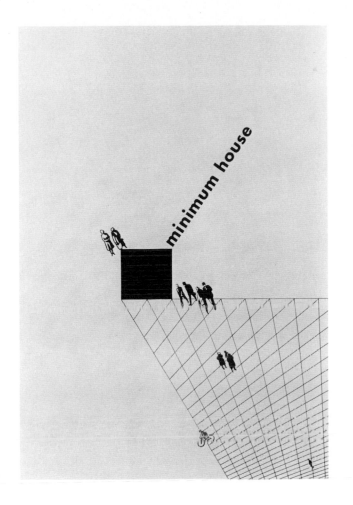

Information poster, 1934. Drawn
directly on the lithography stone,
the design presents a graphic
abstraction of the location of a
new theater. Sutnar consistently
was concerned in his design
with the function of information
transfer.

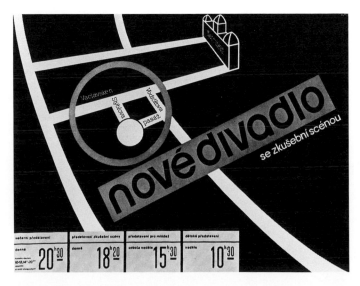

establishing a "full-service" design office: his work included book jackets, toys, furniture, silverware, dishes, fabrics, stage design, and exhibition design. His industrial exhibits in Leipzig (1927) and in Belgrade (1938) are but two examples of his versatility. By 1939 he was referred to as a "graphic editor, graphic planner, graphic architect."[2]

The American Years

In April 1939 the Czechoslovak Department of Education sent Sutnar to New York City to set up the Czechoslovak State Hall, which he had designed for the World's Fair. That same spring saw Hitler's annexation of the Sudetenland and subsequent occupation of most of Czechoslovakia. Sutnar, because of his pre-invasion anti-Nazi activities, was not able to return home and was stranded in the United States, separated from his wife and two young sons until 1946, when he was able to bring them to the United States. The downfall of the Czechoslovak government meant that Sutnar could not complete the exhibit he had been sent to erect. He was, however, able to obtain other project work related to the World's Fair.

Sutnar's next important assignment was for the Research Department of Sweet's Catalog Service. Now a McGraw-Hill Information Systems company, Sweet's has been producing catalogs of industrial and architectural products since 1906. Sutnar was to work for Sweet's for nineteen years, from 1941 to 1960.

Designs and models for the Czechoslovak exhibit at the 1939 World's Fair in New York. This project, although not realized because of the outbreak of World War II, brought Sutnar to the United States, where he remained for the rest of his career.

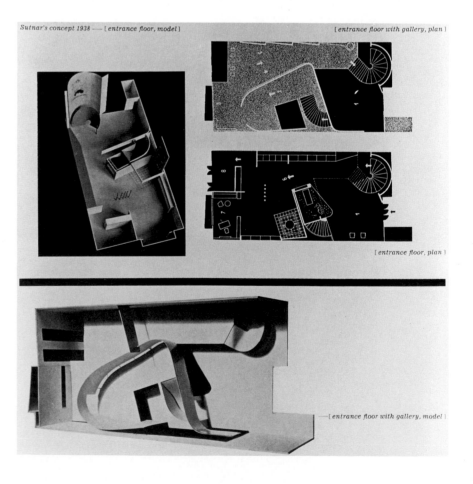

Sutnar's concept 1938 — [entrance floor, model]

[entrance floor with gallery, plan]

[entrance floor, plan]

[entrance floor with gallery, model]

The building boom that followed World War II stimulated the creation of new building-related products and gave rise to a need for information graphics in the industry. Sutnar's skills at applying the "new typography" were exactly what Sweet's needed. He worked in close collaboration with Knut Lonberg-Holm, Sweet's first director of research. Lonberg-Holm, an architect by training, played a central but largely unacknowledged role in the history of design. Buckminster Fuller once commented that it was Lonberg-Holms's photographs of American construction techniques in architecture that excited Walter Gropius and the Bauhaus designers in the years following World War I. It is known that after exposure to these photographs several Bauhaus figures traveled to the United States one by one to see American architectural techniques, which subsequently were evident in the designs of Gropius, Mies van der Rohe, and others.

Together Sutnar and Lonberg-Holm developed the format of Sweet's catalog. Joseph V. Bower, Sweet's present national marketing manager, characterizes their contributions as "just as dramatic a change from previous product information presentation as was the introduction of the International Style [in architecture]. "[3] In 1941 Sutnar was already implementing what were later to be called "corporate graphics standards" in his design program for the circle S trademark and in the organization of Sweet's extensive technical catalog library. He viewed the development of product information standards as an important part of the overall growth of industry in the world. "The need is not only for more factual information," he said, "but for better presentation with the visual clarity and precision gained through new design techniques. Fundamentally this means the development of design patterns capable of transmitting a flow of information."[4] Sutnar saw this information design as a blending of the elements of *function* (making information easy to find, read, comprehend, and remember), *flow* (the rational progression of information for fast perception), and *form* (the line, color, and shape on the page). He applied the principles he had learned from the Bauhaus, Tschichold, and "machine-age" typography. Asymmetric page formats, the frequent use of bleed edges, contrasting weights of Futura types, reverse type, the application of color for smooth visual movement through the text—all these qualities were characteristic of the redesigned Sweet's catalogs. Sutnar's design concepts for the system eventually led to shortened copy segments as well.

Sutnar saw the double-page spread as the visual unit of his plan. He drew the reader's attention first to the upper right-hand corner and then led him to the

Established in 1941, the design
program for Sweet's Catalog
Service was one of Sutnar's
major career projects. Shown
here are variations on the circle
S logo and the series of volumes
in Sweet's library. Sutnar's organization of this vast array of complex technical infomation stands
as a landmark in the history of
graphic design.

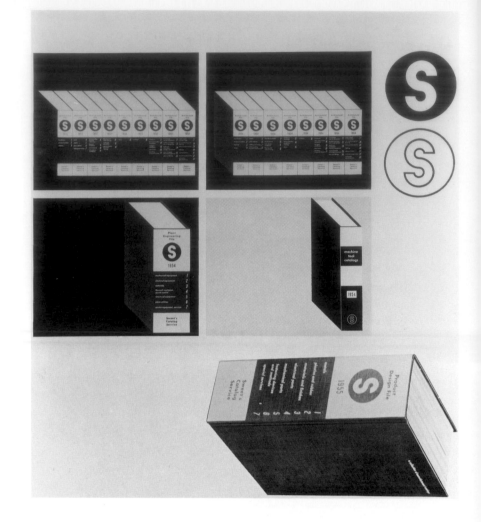

next piece of important information in the spread. Charts and diagrams were

important visual tools in this design scheme, as were the systematically applied

shapes and colors.

Teacher and Writer

Seven years after immigrating to the United States, Sutnar returned to teaching;

as before in Prague, he maintained his design practice at the same time. From

1946 to 1949 he taught design at the Pratt Institute. It was natural that his own

practice and the need to devise problems and learning situations for his students

should give rise to lucid writing about design for a wider audience than the class-

room. In his extensive published work he explained his process of visual organ-

ization and communication. In 1944, in collaboration with Lonberg-Holm, Sutnar

produced *Catalog Design—New Patterns in Product Information* for Sweet's

Catalog Service. This spiral-bound book was promoted by Sweet's as "evaluating

the individual catalog as a dynamic marketing tool and analyzing the basic prob-

lems of catalog design in a wide range of case studies."[5]

In the introduction to *Catalog Design* Sutnar writes that the process of

designing a catalog, like the solving of any other visual problem, is composed of

three distinct phases: "*analysis of the design problem*, setting up new standards for function, content, and format; *the development of standard design elements*; and the *integration of these elements into new design patterns*."[6] The book itself represents a clear statement of these stages of design development, as Sutnar applies the theory to its page layouts, symbols, and photographs.

In a 1947 article for *Interiors* magazine entitled "Design Information," Sutnar and Longberg-Holm generalized the principles from *Catalog Design* for application to a broader range of communications. In 1950 they collaborated on *Catalog Design Progress*; and Sutnar himself published *Design for Point-of-Sale* in 1952 and *Package Design: The Force of Visual Selling* in 1953.

In *Catalog Design Progress* Sutnar and Lonberg-Holm restate their dynamic system of graphics standards devised to facilitate the understanding of product information. Contemporary design examples are compared with those of the past. A Bauhaus-like statement is offered concerning the visual and psychological power of shapes and colors in producing the self-evident image: "For a catalog on plastics, the sphere, cube, and cone support the product's desirable properties: moldability, transparency, colorability."[7] As a book, *Catalog Design Progress* itself is a tour de force. Its charts and diagrams are masterworks of clarity and precision. Its oblong format is distinctive. The free page organization gives emphasis to the horizontal flow of information. Near the end of the book, Sutnar includes a diagram of the design process, which he calls a synthesis of function, flow, and form. In the diagram, design appears between the polar opposites of function and form. According to Sutnar, "the function of design may thus be defined as one of resolving the conflict of such polarities into a new entity."

Design Projects of the 1950s

By 1951 Sutnar was ready to open his own design firm in New York. Over the next decade he completed many important professional assignments. The graphics program for Carr's Self-Service Department Store in New Jersey, done in 1956–1957, had to provide a structure that would be both interesting and quickly understandable in relation to the overwhelming variety of goods on sale. Design controls were developed around a distinguished identity element that appeared on all products. Graphic standards included coordinated layouts, alphabets, and colors. Twenty years later Massimo Vignelli would design a merchandising program for Bloomingdale's reminiscent of the Sutnar program for Carr's.

Sutnar's work for Carr's and for Addo-x Business Machines demonstrated his special capacity for the design of graphic symbols. His symbol system for the Bell Telephone Company remains today a program of high visibility and mean-

Poster number 6 of a ten-poster series, "The Story of Oil," done for Standard Oil of New Jersey, 1943–1950. From a transparency provided by the Exxon Corporation; original dimensions not available.

Pages from *Catalog Design Progress*, designed in 1950 for Sweet's Catalog Service, show the use of grids and bar rules to contain information compactly and with clarity. The grids are black, and the text is in color.

From *Catalog Design Progress*, this "structural organization" diagram facilitates the job of designing a 20-page service catalog on electrical wires and cables.

Diagram and sample catalog page from *Catalog Design Progress*, indicating how simple shapes, symbols, and color can create impact and visual control.

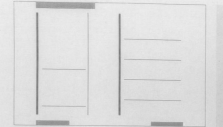

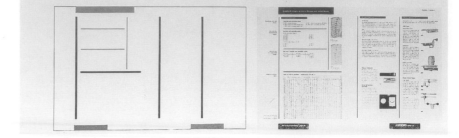

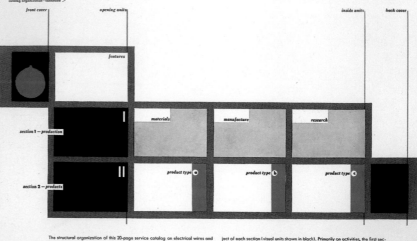

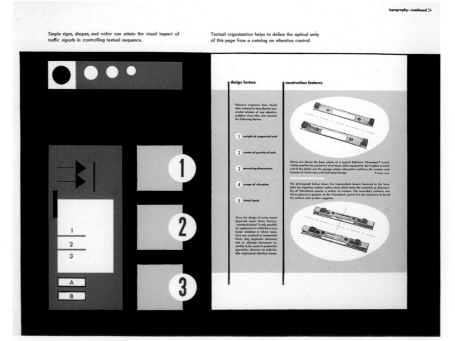

ing. Sutnar's identity elements were pioneering efforts in an area of design that is now accepted as commonplace. "A company without a distinctive house style is like a person with a pale personality," he liked to say.

In 1959, as art director for *Theatre Arts* magazine, he completely redesigned its format. The fifties also saw his extensive graphics campaign for Knoll + Drake furniture. Sutnar's challenge was to combine the existing, well-known Knoll *K* mark with the *D* from Drake in a way that would preserve the integrity of each while creating a new form that could be easily read and remembered. Of Sutnar's work during these years, Allon Schoener, writer and design consultant, said, "In a period when most designers cultivate an anonymous versatility, the work of Ladislav Sutnar stands apart: Sutnar has carved out a style so much his own that no one quite dares to imitate it."[8]

Visual Design in Action

Schoener collaborated with Sutnar in 1961 on the exhibit "Visual Design in Action" for the Contemporary Arts Center in Cincinnati and the American Institute of Graphic Arts. Sutnar's book by the same title, published in 1961 as well, is the definitive expression of his methodology and work.

Visual Design in Action is organized in three sections. The first addresses principles or attributes of design, beginning with visual interest. Visual interest is, says Sutnar, "a force of inventive design which will excite and hold attention on the objective. Visual interest draws [viewers] into the process and seeks their participation by arousing their curiosity."[9] In the case of marketing applications, the visual interest must be translated into actual buying action by the consumer.

The second attribute of design is visual simplicity. Sutnar defines this as "less is more or the power of a simple design to communicate directly"; he quotes Lewis Mumford as having remarked that "less is more only when it is recognized that the more one eliminates, the greater is the importance of refining that which remains."[10] All visual messages should be reduced to their most direct, basic elements. Precision and ordering are two means to achieve visual simplicity, which, in turn, enhances the process of locating, reading, and comprehending information.

Visual continuity, the third attribute of design, is also called by Sutnar "perpetual continuity in unity."[11] An example of this would be a magazine in which two pages are seen as a unit of a sequential progression of spreads. Visual continuity involves the careful coordination of all design functions in a pattern that provides a smooth visual flow for fast reading and comprehension. It pro-

Small-scale advertisements for
Addo-x Business Machines, from
1956–1959.

Examples of applications for
Carr's Self-Service Department
Store in New Jersey, designed
by Sutnar in 1956–1957. The
design had to support the store's
special approach to merchandising and provide a disciplined
structure that would be rapidly
understandable and interesting.

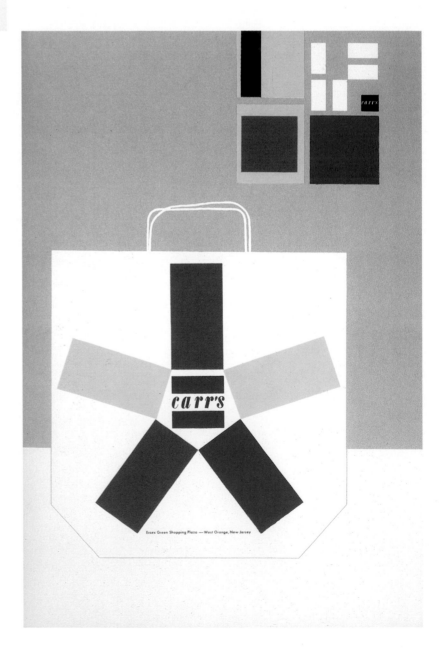

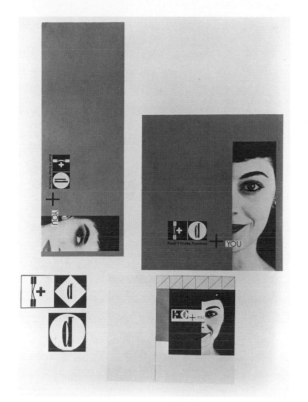

Graphics for the Knoll + Drake Furniture Company, 1954–1955. Sutnar's identity elements were pioneering efforts in a field of design that is now taken for granted. Here the challenge was to combine the existing, well known Knoll *K* with the *D* from Drake in a way that preserved the integrity of each while creating a new, memorable form.

This posterlike counter display for Vera scarves, from 1958–1959, shows Sutnar's skill at integrating a logo into a larger promotional program. Color.

Cover for *Theatre Arts* magazine, July 1960. The bold integration of photography and flat color activates the composition.

Diagram from *Visual Design in Action*, showing the role of design as a means of resolving such polar opposites as form and function. Color.

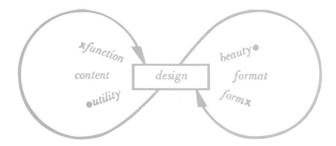

vides rhythm, direction, climax, and yet a unity in the whole piece. Implicit in visual continuity are both visual interest and visual simplicity. These three attributes should be seen as necessary, in differing proportions, for any problem dealing with the flow of information. Sutnar saw them as fundamental in achieving a distinctive look or house style for any organization or product.

The second section of *Visual Design in Action* is devoted to the presentation of a series of case studies—projects completed by Sutnar for Addo-x, Knoll + Drake, Vera, Sweet's, Carr's, *Theatre Arts*, and others. Color portfolios demonstrate the realization of Sutnar's principles in advertising, business papers, direct mail, industrial catalogs, exhibits and displays, design for education, magazines, book design, signs, symbol, and information design. The third and final section traces the emergence of the modern design concept through a showing of Sutnar's formative works done in Europe between 1929 and 1938.

Sutnar's personal symbol, used on the cover of his book *Visual Design in Action*, published in 1961. Color.

An Integrated Designer

Physically a slight man, formal in his bearing, always dressed in suit and tie, Sutnar channeled his extraordinary energy into work above all else. He was exacting in his demands upon himself and others.

From the beginning to the end of his career, Sutnar always gave some of his time to painting, and from the early 1960s on, he was a painter almost exclusively. The result of this late activity is a body of paintings called "Venus: Joy-Art," reminiscent of Tom Wesselmann's mid-1960s "Great American Nude" series. Like Wesselmann's nudes, Sutnar's flat-pattern Venuses were increasingly erotic prototypes of women in a variety of moods and situations.

Throughout his life Sutnar recalled the years in Prague as the most successful of his career, probably because in his own estimation he never quite accommodated himself to living in the United States. In many ways Sutnar remained a foreigner in a country that continued to seem alien to him. Nonetheless, he produced a body of work that earned him numerous national and international awards[12] and a solid reputation for being able to use visual design discoveries and techniques to synthesize art, science, and technology for business and industry. Mildred Constantine observed, in her preface to his *Visual Design in Action*, "There is a force and meaningful consistency in Sutnar's entire body of work, which permits him to express himself with a rich diversity in exhibition design and the broad variations of graphic design. Sutnar has the assured stature of the integrated designer."

Sutnar Chronology

1897
Born in Pilsen, Czechoslovakia

c. 1910–c. 1920
Student at Academy of Industrial Art, Charles University, and Technical University, Prague

1923–1939
Professor of design, State School of Graphic Arts, Prague

1929–1939
Art director at Druzstevni Prace publishing firm

1929
Gold medal, World Exhibition, Barcelona

1932–1939
Director of State School of Graphic Arts, Prague

1937
Grands prix and gold medals, Exposition Internationale d 'Art et Techniques de la vie Moderne, Paris

1939
Designer of Czechoslovak pavilion at the New York World's Fair; remains in United States

1941–1960
Art director, Research Department, Sweet's Catalog Service

1942–1969
Design consultant to many firms

1950
Coauthor and designer of *Catalog Design Progress* for Sweet's Catalog Service

1951
Establishes his own design firm in New York

1956–1959
Designs for Addo-x

1961
Publishes *Visual Design in Action*

1971
Inducted into Hall of Fame of the New York Art Directors Club

1976
Dies in New York

Bradbury Thompson 1911–

James Bradbury Thompson was born in Topeka, Kansas, on March 25, 1911, the fourth child of James Kay Thompson, an auditor for the Atchison, Topeka, and Santa Fe Railroad (and a nationally known breeder, exhibitor, and judge of prize-winning poultry), and Eunice Bradbury Thompson. Mrs. Thompson died when her son was only seven months old. Her mother, the wife of a distinguished pioneer minister, came to live in the home and help raise the boy and his three older sisters. His grandmother, along with several aunts who also helped look after him, encouraged the inclination toward the visual arts that Bradbury Thompson showed early in life.

Though hardly a major cultural center in the early 1900s, Topeka did possess a strong public library system, and the Thompson family library contained many good books.[1] Bradbury Thompson had developed an interest in book design and typography by the time he was in junior high school. During his last year in junior high he was asked to join the drafting staff in the civil engineering office of H. A. Marshall, who was also his Sunday school teacher. This design work continued through Thompson's years in college and gave him valuable practical experience.

High school provided new opportunities: here Thompson took art courses, including one in mechanical drawing, and was both art editor of the school paper and designer of the yearbook. In 1929 he enrolled at Washburn University in Topeka, majoring in economics and minoring in art. He was editor and designer of the undergraduate yearbook in 1932 and 1934 and distinguished himself in track, with a dash record that lasted eighteen years. After classes, he continued to work as a draftsman at the civil engineering office. In addition to the university's library, two of his Washburn art courses made particularly strong impressions: an art appreciation course taught by John Canaday and a drawing course taught by James Gilbert.

Thompson's natural curiosity had led him to discover what he called "the good magazines" — *Gebrauchsgraphik* from Germany; *Vogue*, *Vanity Fair*, and *Harper's Bazaar* from New York. M. F. Agha's experimental graphic work in *Vanity Fair*, especially his use of sans serif type along with classic typefaces, influenced Thompson's yearbook designs. In connection with the yearbooks he also learned much through his work with the Steves Printing Company, a letterpress shop located in Topeka. Steves was the classic family-operated business: Guy was the manager, his wife, Maude, was the secretary, brother Roy was pressman, brother Jay was on the stone, son Harold ran the Linotype machine, and brother Bob ran

Cover of the Washburn College publication *KAW*, Autumn 1933, designed by then-undergraduate Thompson. The placement of the camera lens and the text on a diagonal axis contributes visual excitement to the composition. Color 7″ × 10″.

Cover for *Photo-Engravers Bulletin*, December 1935. The vantage point from which the toy soldier and "Noel" are viewed suggests the coming wartime aerial reconnaissance. Color; 6¼″ × 9¼″.

the bindery. Thompson involved himself in all phases of typography, printing, and production, with the friendly toleration of the Steves family.

For nearly five years after his graduation from Washburn in 1934, Thompson remained in Topeka, designing magazines and yearbooks for Capper Publications. This large firm had sophisticated equipment, its own engraving plant, and two kindly staff artists who were a source of further practical training. Thompson traveled all over Kansas, advising the editors of high school and college yearbooks on design and production.

During this period Thompson was to gain national recognition for his work. Each month, the American Photo-Engravers Association selected a cover for its *Photo-Engravers Bulletin* from those submitted in an open competition, and at the end of the year a winner was chosen among these. Thompson's December 1935 cover design won first prize that year. The $100 cash award "was four weeks' salary for me in 1935," notes Thompson. "I won the contest and the piece still looks presentable to me."[2] During the 1930s this competition was a gateway for such other young designers as Lester Beall, who was working in Chicago at the time.

The Move to New York City

In 1938, at the age of twenty-seven, Thompson left America's heartland and ventured to the East Coast to seek new professional challenges. He stopped off in Chicago, where he met William Kittridge, a distinguished art director at the Lakeside Press. Kittridge was impressed with young Thompson's portfolio and provided him with letters of introduction to seven influential individuals and organizations in the New York design world, including Alexey Brodovitch, art director at *Harper's Bazaar*; Gilbert Tompkins, an artists' agent who represented A. M. Cassandre and Paolo Garretto; and Merton Griswold, of the highly respected printing firm of Rogers-Kellogg-Stillson.

Thompson also visited M. F. Agha at Condé Nast. Although he admired Agha's work, he concluded from his interviews that at Condé Nast he would find less opportunity for creative freedom than at Rogers-Kellogg-Stillson, producer of, among other things, the impressive *Westvaco Inspirations*, a deluxe publication for printers.

His interviews concluded, Thompson returned to Kansas. Two months later, on the same weekend, he received offers from both Condé Nast and Rogers-Kellogg-Stillson. He accepted the latter's.

Westvaco Inspirations

"My first day of working at Rogers-Kellogg-Stillson, a man named Charles Folks came in with a blank dummy and said, 'Here, do *Westvaco Inspirations.*' I knew that RKS had started the magazine many years before, and I was hoping they'd ask me to do it. From then on, for twenty-four years, I designed the majority of the issues."[3] In all, Thompson designed sixty-one issues of *Westvaco Inspirations* between 1939 and 1962.

Westvaco Inspirations was a graphic arts publication issued by the Westvaco Corporation, formerly named the West Virginia Pulp and Paper Company, with the objective of showing typography, photography, art work, and other graphic inventiveness on papers manufactured at its mills. The magazine was printed on both letterpress and lithography. Thompson and the corporation's leaders were in accord in believing that such a publication should be a living example of good graphics. From its founding in 1925 until its discontinuation in 1962, *Westvaco Inspirations* was a leading corporate contributor to graphic design. It remains unsurpassed as an example of promotional graphics.

The Westvaco advertising director reserved the right, in the early years of Thompson's work on the magazine, to decide upon a painting for the cover of each issue. Aside from this, Thompson had no constraints except financial ones. The budget limited him mainly to borrowed plates and separations of graphic work from publications, and the elements of the typecase and print shop. Like Alvin Lustig after him, he found plenty of scope here. "The printing press and the print shop were my canvas, easel, and second studio," he would later declare.[4] Early issues manifested Thompson's interest in publication and advertising art, whereas the later ones tended to emphasize the fine arts.

Westvaco Inspirations became a showcase for Thompson's innovative ideas. In a 1945 issue he brought out his "Monalphabet." In 1950 he presented "Alphabet 26," which combined upper and lowercase letters. Later issues would be filled with engravings gleaned from one of Thompson's most cherished possessions, the 28-volume *Encyclopédie* of Denis Diderot, published in the mideighteenth century. Thompson often took printing plates apart to make new designs, surprinting them in color. He would enlarge letterforms to great scale and use them to create patterns and textures. He made extensive use of "found" images, combining them in collages that were playful and yet perfectly controlled.

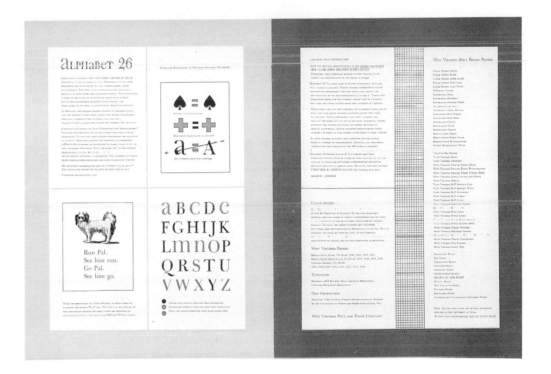

"Monalphabet," *Westvaco Inspirations*, vol. 152, 1945. Each letter in Thompson's sans serif type design has only one form, rather than a capital and a lowercase form. Color. Courtesy Westvaco Corporation.

"Alphabet 26," *Westvaco Inspirations*, vol. 180, 1950. Another simplified alphabet in which each letter has only one form. Color. Courtesy Westvaco Corporation.

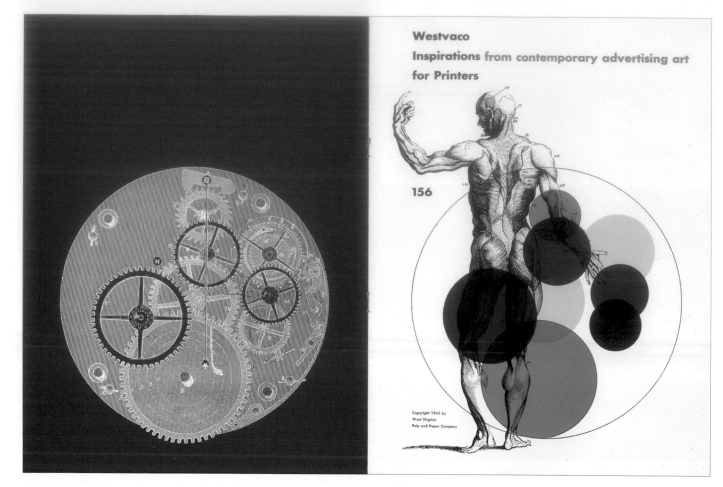

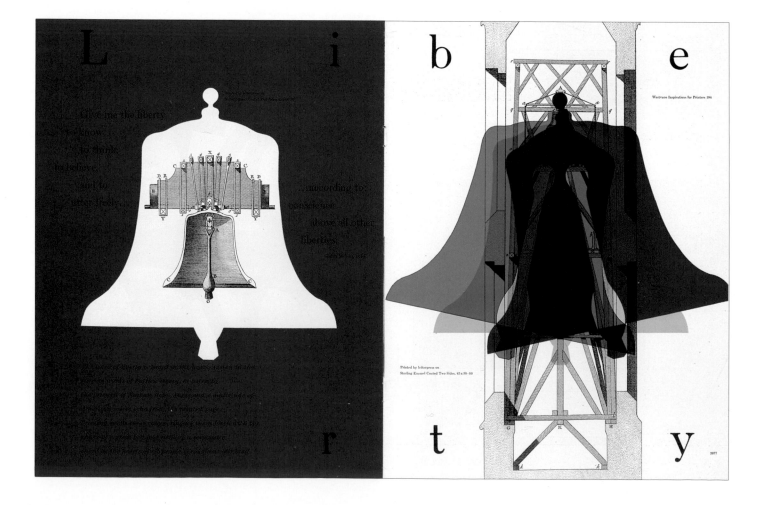

Spread from *Westvaco Inspirations*, vol. 156, 1945. Between 1939 and 1962 Thompson designed sixty-one issues of this promotional magazine, published by the Westvaco paper company. Budget constraints limited him to borrowed plates and separations from other publications, and the elements of the typecase. "The printing press and the print shop were my canvas, easel, and second studio," he later said. The magazine's page dimensions were 9" × 12". Courtesy Westvaco Corporation.

Spread from *Westvaco Inspirations*, vol. 194, 1953. Courtesy Westvaco Corporation.

Spread from *Westvaco Inspirations*, vol. 177, 1949. Courtesy Westvaco Corporation.

Spread from *Westvaco Inspirations*, vol. 192, 1953. Courtesy Westvaco Corporation.

Spread from *Westvaco Inspirations*, vol. 210, 1958. Courtesy Westvaco Corporation.

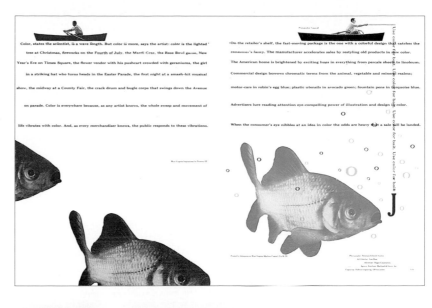

Other Magazine Work

From 1942 to 1945 Thompson was associate chief of the Overseas Branch Art Section of the Office of War Information. Fortunately the office was located in New York, and Thompson was able to carry on his work with *Westvaco Inspirations* at night and on weekends. Working closely with Tobias Moss, formerly on the staff of *Life* magazine, he designed two wartime periodicals, *Victory* and *USA*. Created to communicate the good American life, these magazines were produced in various languages and dropped behind enemy lines.

Another colleague at the Office of War Information was Cyrilly Abels, who, immediately after the war, became managing editor of *Mademoiselle*. She, along with the editor, Betsy Talbot Blackwell, offered Thompson a position as art director of this youth-oriented fashion magazine, which was to become his base for the next fifteen years. Thompson's eye-catching *Mademoiselle* covers stood out from the competition on the newsstand and made him a designer of national reputation.

In 1945, too, on the recommendation of M. F. Agha, Thompson took on the design direction of *Art News* and *Art News Annual*, a responsibility he held for twenty-seven years. In 1967 he created the original format for *Smithsonian* magazine — a format so successful that it has not changed in subsequent years. Another important redesign project was for *Progressive Architecture* in 1971. In the issue that introduced the new format, the magazine reported to its readers that Thompson had "borrowed from two of the key elements of today's architectural scene — systems construction and computer technology. *Progressive Architecture*'s new look is based on a rigid framework that allows for a large number of variables; layouts are built within the framework by combining varying elements. Type is set by computer. The larger page size will enhance editorial material and allow a better display of photographs and graphics."[5] All together, Thompson has designed or redesigned nearly three dozen magazines.

Designing the American Classics

From the late 1950s through the 1970s Thompson's work, both with periodicals and with books, showed a greater inclination toward classic principles. He sought legibility with flush-left typographic asymmetry that made use of classic type styles. This shift is evident in his designs for the Library of American Classics, a series of books published by Westvaco and sent as Christmas gifts to customers and corporate friends. The first volume appeared in 1958.

Cover for *USA*, vol. 2, no. 7 (1940). During World War II Thompson designed both *USA* and *Victory*, propaganda magazines put out by the American government and dropped behind enemy lines. Color; 5⅜" × 8".

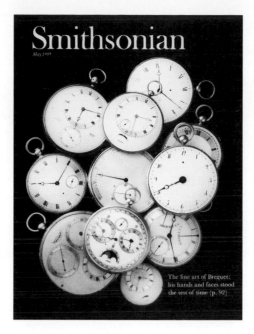

Cover for *Smithsonian*, May 1985. Thompson's classical design for this magazine, introduced in 1967, has stood the test of time. Color; 8¼″ × 11″.

As art director at *Mademoiselle* after World War II, Thompson brought the fashion magazine to a new height of visual elegance. With Agha and Brodovitch, Thompson was a leader in introducing new visual concepts to the consumer magazine. This cover is from *Mademoiselle's* February 1950 issue. Color; 8½″ × 11½″.

Cover for *Mademoiselle*, April 1952. Color; 8½″ × 11¼″.

Cover for *Art News*, Summer 1970. Thompson's design features an image by Henri Matisse. Color; 9⅜″ × 12¼″.

Each 5¾″ by 9½″ book in the series has its own character, although all the editions come with slipcases, head bands, and other features of fine book making. Every volume has a foreword explaining the book designer's concepts for that particular work. Thompson carefully integrates typography, illustrative material, and fine papers to create a harmony between the visual and verbal elements.

The first in the series was Washington Irving's *The Legend of Sleepy Hollow*. It was followed by such titles as *The Celebrated Jumping Frog of Calaveras County*, by Mark Twain, O. Henry's *The Four Million*, and Herman Melville's *Typee*. One of Thompson's favorites is *American Cookery*, by Amelia Simmons, originally published in 1796. Here, as with the other Classics, Thompson's design captures the character of the time in which the book was first printed. Thompson has respected the choices of the original printer by repeating Baskerville types and the long *s* letter. He has made the book more accessible to modern readers, however, by inserting side headings in italics and varied sectional headings taken from the transitional sentences of the author. He uses as illustrations a number of copperplate engravings from an encyclopedia of 1797. His addition of subtle color enhances the flow of the book.

Another distinctive volume is *Daisy Miller*, by Henry James, in which Thompson uses paintings by J. M. Whistler and J. S. Sargent. The lines of spoken text are broken at the ends of phrases, a technique employed also in the Washburn College Bible. A collection of Benjamin Franklin's writings shows even more typographic experimentation, with large type making a powerful pattern on the page. The bold bleed of Thompson's favorite engravings from Diderot's *Encyclopédie* balances the pages of patterned text matter to create an effective visual rhythm. In *The Red Badge of Courage*, by Stephen Crane, a simulated bullet hole and splatters of blood penetrate the volume.

The first book in the Classics series was printed in an edition of 2,500; by 1964 the run had increased to 12,000. The collection stands as an excellent example of the balancing of the traditional and the experimental.

In 1968 Thompson produced a volume for Westvaco integrating the graphic concepts of sixteen distinguished international book designers, including himself. Entitled *Homage to the Book*, this work has become a popular reference in book design.

Title spread from *The Red Badge of Courage*, by Stephen Crane, Westvaco Library of American Classics, 1968. Thompson simulates spattered blood and a progressively smaller bullet hole that penetrates most of the book. Color; 5¾″ × 9½″. Courtesy Westvaco Corporation.

This cover and slipcase for *Typee*, by Herman Melville, printed in 1962 as part of the Westvaco Library of American Classics, shows Thompson's attention to matching the theme of a literary classic with appropriate typography and illustrations. Color; 5¾″ × 9½″. Courtesy Westvaco Corporation.

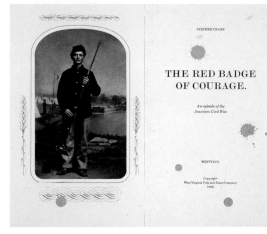

Title page and inside spread from *American Cookery*, by Amelia Simmons, Westvaco Library of American Classics, 1963. Thompson provides an elegantly contemporary presentation of a 1796 cookbook and follows the choice of the book's original printer by using Baskerville types and the long *s* letters. The illustrations are engravings taken from an encyclopedia of 1797. Color; 5¾" × 9½". Courtesy Westvaco Corporation.

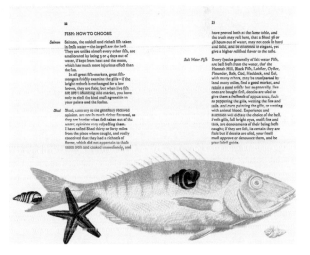

Sixteen Designers

Homage to
the Book

Leonard Baskin
Joseph Blumenthal
Bert Clarke
Brooke Crutchley
Alvin Eisenman
Norman Ives
Joseph Low
Giovanni Mardersteig
Herbert Matter
Paul Rand
Roderick Stinehour
Bradbury Thompson
Georg Trump
Jan Tschichold
Carl Zahn
Hermann Zapf

Foreword by Frederick B. Adams, Jr.

Westvaco

Homage to the Book, produced by Westvaco in 1968, is a beautifully packaged set of folios by sixteen of the world's outstanding book designers. Thompson coordinated the project and designed this title page. Color; 9" × 12". Courtesy Westvaco Corporation.

Pitney Bowes 1976 Annual Report

Annual report cover for Pitney
Bowes, 1976. Business graphics
have been an important application for Thompson's abilities, and
his example has drawn other
designers into this field. Color;
8½" × 11".

Consultant to Corporations, Designer of Postage Stamps

Over the years Thompson has served as design consultant to numerous organizations, including Cornell University, the Harvard Business School, the
Menninger Foundation, The Ford Motor Company, Pitney–Bowes, Famous Artists
Schools, McGraw-Hill, and Time-Life Books. For Time-Life he designed the formats for *The Library of Art* and *Foods of the World*. For Ford he created a large
publication entitled *Freedom of the American Road*, which presented sugges-
tions for way to improve highways and driving in the nation.

In 1958 he received his first commission to design a stamp for the United
States Postal Service. He has since produced over ninety stamps, more than any
other designer in America. Thompson has been a member of the Citizens' Stamp
Advisory Committee since 1969 and in this capacity has brought other gifted
designers into service. His suggestion that a USA logo be used on each stamp
has given unity to the stamp program.

The Washburn College Bible

Thompson started work in 1969 on an immense project that would consume
much of his energy over the next ten years and would become the most important achievement of his long career. The Washburn College Bible began as an
undertaking of the Field Enterprises Educational Corporation, for which
Thompson designed several books and redesigned the *Chicago Daily News*
during the 1960s. Field Enterprises asked him to design a new Bible and gave
him full control over the project, with no preliminary limitations.

Thompson arranged the 1,800 pages of text in phrases, for ease of reading.
He used masterworks of art, selected by J. Carter Brown, Director of the National
Gallery of Art, as dividers between sections. Josef Albers, then his colleague
on the faculty at Yale University, created screen prints to serve as frontispieces
for the Bible's three volumes.

When the economic recession of 1973–1975 forced Field Enterprises to
abandon the Bible project, Thompson made up his mind to find a new sponsor
himself. After visiting publishers, foundations, and granting agencies without success, he turned to a friend who sat with him on the board of trustees of his alma
mater, Washburn University. The trustees, with the leadership of Ruth Garvey
Fink and Olive White Garvey, were persuaded to take on the project.

Art News, 1970

Cover for *Freedom of the American Road*, a book on highways and driving conditions, and how to improve them, published by the Ford Motor Company. Color; 10½″ × 13″.

This Week is a Sunday newspaper supplement. Thompson used transportation signs to introduce articles about cars in this cover from October 11, 1964. Color; 10¾″ × 12¾″.

Society of Illustrators, 1960

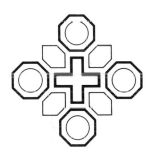

Washburn College Bible, 1979

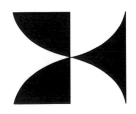

College at SUNY, Purchase, 1970

Westvaco, Corporation, 1968

Three samples from the over ninety stamps Thompson has designed for the U.S. Postal Service. Shown are a commemorative stamp from 1980 featuring a painting by Josef Albers, a stamp designed in 1982 to honor America's libraries featuring six antique engraved letters, and

Two-page spread from the
Washburn College Bible, 1979.
The painting is *Adam and Eve in
the Garden of Eden*, by Peter
Paul Rubens and Jan Brueghel
the Elder, from c. 1620. The
page at right shows the use
of the Sabon Antiqua type for
headings and in the "phrased
line" text. 9¾" × 14".

The First Book of Moses called Genesis

Genesis

1:1 In the beginning
God created the heaven and the earth.
2 And the earth was without form, and void;
and darkness was upon the face of the deep.
And the Spirit of God
moved upon the face of the waters.

3 And God said,
Let there be light:
and there was light.
4 And God saw the light, that it was good:
and God divided the light from the darkness.
5 And God called the light Day,
and the darkness he called Night.
And the evening and the morning
were the first day.

6 And God said,
Let there be a firmament
in the midst of the waters,
and let it divide the waters from the waters.
7 And God made the firmament,
and divided the waters
which were under the firmament
from the waters
which were above the firmament:
and it was so.

8 And God called the firmament Heaven.
And the evening and the morning
were the second day.

9 And God said,
Let the waters under the heaven
be gathered together unto one place,
and let the dry land appear:
and it was so.
10 And God called the dry land Earth;
and the gathering together of the waters
called he Seas:
and God saw that it was good.
11 And God said,
Let the earth bring forth grass,
the herb yielding seed,
and the fruit tree yielding fruit after his kind,
whose seed is in itself, upon the earth:
and it was so.
12 And the earth brought forth grass,
and herb yielding seed after his kind,
and the tree yielding fruit,
whose seed was in itself, after his kind:
and God saw that it was good.

The Washburn College Bible, in three volumes, was printed in 1979 in an edition of only 398 copies. Type was set by a computer program, with refinements introduced by Thompson. The typeface used was Sabon Antiqua (in 14-point size), Claude Garamond's design of 1532 as refined by Jan Tschichold in 1967. The same type size is used throughout, for text, headings, and captions. In awarding Thompson a medal for his Bible in 1986, the Type Directors Club of New York pronounced it the "most thorough reassessment of the printed Bible format since Gutenberg."

Thompson the Teacher

In 1956 Thompson was invited by Alvin Eisenman, head of graphic design studies at Yale University, to become a visiting critic for the graduate design program there. Eisenman had previously obtained the services of Alexey Brodovitch and Alvin Lustig in the same role, understanding well the benefit students could derive from contact with practicing designers. Thompson continues teaching at Yale today. He owes his longevity in the job to this capacity for true exchange with students: "That's the greatest experience—to expose your ignorance to young people. . . . And young people are such wonderful things. You can teach them so much. And learn so much."[6]

An American Original

One of the most prolific magazine and book designers of the twentieth century, Thompson has exerted a powerful influence on the style of contemporary graphic design. His work has a peculiarly American quality; the designer Allen Hurlburt compared its improvisation and its unification of many disparate elements into a rhythmic pattern with Gershwin's translations of the jazz music of his period. Thompson was by no means unaffected by European design, however. In the 1930s he studied the work of the European practitioners of Dada, Futurism, and Constructivism and internalized a thorough understanding of typographic modernism. He learned to use the visual contours of words or sentences to create pictures and illustrate ideas. As was true with much of the work of the European avant-garde, the content and form of Thompson's images were necessary to each other. Herbert Bayer's alphabet design for the Bauhaus has been credited with influencing Thompson in a similar direction in the 1940s.

Thompson's is a design approach that emphasizes human values, human scale, and functionalism. In a speech delivered in 1959 on the subject of printing technology as it affects the designer, he said, "It is continually important to remain masters of the machine. Most of all it is essential to strive for a simple artistic integrity and the idealistic standards that have always been essential in making the printed word useful and pleasing to other people." Nonetheless, "we must keep pace with new scientific developments in printing, such as electronic methods of typesetting and platemaking and high-speed methods of presswork which exceed the most fantastic imagination of our predecessors."[7]

Thompson's definition of graphic design is "the interfusion of word and image. But of the two, typography is the most important part."[8] In 1956 he wrote:

Type can be a tool, a toy and a teacher;
it can provide a means of livelihood,
a hobby for relaxation,
an intellectual stimulant,
and a spiritual satisfaction.

I believe an avid interest in Type
necessarily includes a zest
for everyday life.[9]

His interest in typography as a visual element is always balanced with a keen awareness of the technical side of typesetting and production. In the decade between 1970 and 1980 Thompson produced a series of books in which he employed a cold-type composition process; even trained typographers have difficulty distinguishing the results from what would have been achieved with metal type.

Although Thompson's work has been experimental in quality, there has also been a consistent interest in classicism. Like Tschichold, Rogers, and Gill, he has been drawn particularly to the achievements in typography of the sixteenth century in France. These influences can be seen in Thompson's use of the Garamond, Sabon, Jenson, and Baskerville typefaces.

"Whether we are examining his precise cropping and careful placing of images on the printed page or studying his attention to typographic detail," wrote Allen Hurlburt in 1980, "we come away impressed by his sense of order and structure."[10] Thompson's functional design, with its clear preference for mechanically derived over hand-drawn form, is never dry or boring, however. Rather, he is able to convey his own inventive and playful spirit while maintaining discipline and clarity.

The center of Thompson's creative activity has for some years been the studio compactly set in a bay window at one end of the master bedroom in his Riverside, Connecticut, home. Thompson has always used elements from his personal past and present in his graphic work. A famous spread from *Westvaco Inspirations*, showing a cross section of a fishing scene, came from a drawing done by one of his daughters, aged seven. "When I looked at her drawing," Thompson later recalled, "it broke a barrier for me and I visualized the possibility of seeing above and below the water at the same time."[11] Another well-known spread, often referred to as the Westvaco Mask, came from a drawing made by another of his children when she was six.

"Thompson's song," wrote Eugene Ettenberg in 1955, "has a bounce and an interplay of many rhythms."[12] He blends the new with the old, complexity with simplicity, word with image, in ways that are unexpected, often humorous, but never capricious. He never loses track of his own stated goal, that of "making the printed word useful and pleasing to other people."

Bradbury Thompson, 1986. Photograph by R. Roger Remington.

Thompson Chronology

1911
Born in Topeka, Kansas

1929-1934
Attends Washburn College, Topeka; designs and edits Washburn College yearbook

1934-1938
Designer at Capper Publications, Topeka

1938
Moves to New York

1938-1942
Art director at Rogers-Kellogg-Stillson printing firm

1939-1962
Designer and editor of *Westvaco Inspirations*

1942-1945
Associate chief, Office of War Information, New York

1945
Designs "Monalphabet," a simplified alphabet

1945-1959
Art director at *Mademoiselle* magazine

1945-1972
Design director at *Art News* and *Art News Annual*

1950
Designs "Alphabet 26," a simplified alphabet

1952-
Design consultant to Westvaco Corporation

1956-
Faculty member, Graphic Design Studies, Yale University

1958-
Designs Westvaco Library of American Classics

1959-1975
Design consultant for Pitney Bowes and McGraw-Hill Publications

1965
Receives Doctor of Fine Arts honorary degree from Washburn University

1965-
Special projects for Smithsonian Institution, Harvard Business School, Cornell University, Field Enterprises Educational Corporation

1969-1979
Designs Washburn College Bible

1969
Member of Citizens' Stamp Advisory Committee, U.S. Postal Service

1975
Receives Gold Medal from American Institute of Graphic Arts

1977
Elected to Hall of Fame of New York Art Directors Club

1983
Receives Doctor of Fine Arts honorary degree from Rhode Island School of Design and Frederic W. Goudy Award, Rochester Institute of Technology

1986
Medalist, Type Directors Club of New York

1986
Award for Continuing Excellence, Society of Publication Designers

Notes

Preface

1. Humphrey Carpenter, *W. H. Auden, A Biography* (Boston: Houghton Mifflin, 1982), p. xvi.

2. University of Rochester, *Proceedings of the Creation Conference* (Rochester, New York, 1987), n.p.

3. Robert Jensen, *Ivan Chermayeff: A Design Anatomy* (Minneapolis: Walker Art Center, 1979), p. 5.

4. Joseph H. Cator, *The Utopian Vision of Moholy-Nagy* (Ann Arbor: University of Michigan Research Press, 1904), p. xvii.

An American School

1. Interview with Aaron Burns, New York, New York, 22 May 1987.

2. Interview with Louis Dorfsman, New York, New York, 22 May 1987.

3. Lorraine Wild, "Modern American Graphics II: The Birth of a Profession," *Industrial Design*, July/August 1983, p. 56.

4. Interview with Mildred Constantine, New York, New York, 19 March 1987.

5. Interview with Louis Dorfsman.

6. Judith Wittenberg, "The Romance of Scholarship," *Simmons Review*, Fall 1986, p. 5.

M. F. Agha

1. In one of his many articles written for *Vogue*, Agha, with tongue in cheek, slips his own name into a listing of famous people for whom 1896 was significant: "The year of grace 1896 was a year positively studded with events of tremendous importance to the progress of Good Taste. William Morris died that year — a loss to the world of Arts only partially compensated for by the fact that M. F. Agha was born the same year. It was in 1896 that the sinuous lines of a style called 'Art Nouveau' by the Germans and 'Les nouilles en délire' ['the noodles in frenzy'] by the French first appeared on the architectural horizon. It was during that year that G. B. Shaw took colour photographs, Aubrey Beardsley illustrated *The Rape of the Lock*, and Oscar Wilde was clapped in jail." M. F. Agha, "S. Melies: Father of the Impossible," *Vogue*, 15 May 1939, p. 68.

2. Gertrude Snyder, "Pro.File: Dr. M. F. Agha," *Upper and Lower Case* 3 (December 1976), p. 5.

3. Caroline Seebohm, *The Man Who Was Vogue: The Life and Times of Condé Nast* (New York: Viking Press, 1982), p. 228.

4. Frank Crowninshield, "The Hegira of Mehemed," *PM* 5 (August-September 1939), n.p.

5. M. F. Agha, "Leave European Art in Europe," *Advertising Arts*, January 1932, p. 15.

6. M. F. Agha, "An Art Director," Agha Papers: The Joyce Morrow Collection, Rochester Institute of Technology, n.p.

7. "Mehemed Fehmy Agha (Dr. M. F. Agha)," *Annual of the New York Art Directors Club*, 1972, n.p.

8. Seebohm, *The Man Who Was Vogue*, p. 234.

9. Interview with Cipe Pineles, New York, New York, 21 November 1985.

10. William Golden, "The Man Who Knew Too Much," *PM* 5 (August-September 1939), n.p.

11. Crowninshield, "The Hegira of Mehemed," n.p.

12. M. F. Agha, "Ralph Steiner," *Creative Arts*, January 1932, p. 35.

13. Interview with Joyce Morrow, Paoli, Pennsylvania, 17 January 1986.

14. Snyder, "Pro.File: Dr. M. F. Agha," p. 5.

15. Snyder, "Pro.File: Dr. M. F. Agha," p. 5.

16. "Mehemed Fehmy Agha (Dr. M. F. Agha)," *Annual of the New York Art Directors Club*, 1972, n.p.

17. Snyder, "Pro.File: Dr. M. F. Agha," p. 5.

18. Condé Nast, "Dr. Agha in Berlin," *PM* 5 (August-September 1939), n.p.

19. Snyder, "Pro.File: Dr. M. F. Agha," p. 5.

20. Snyder, "Pro.File: Dr. M. F. Agha," p. 5.

21. Snyder, "Pro.File: Dr. M. F. Agha," p. 5.

22. Seebohm, *The Man Who Was Vogue*, pp. 206–207.

23. *American Printer*, March 1935, n.p.

24. Interview with Cipe Pineles.

25. Seebohm, *The Man Who Was Vogue*, p. 231.

26. M. F. Agha, "On Magazines," *AIGA Journal of Graphic Design*, Fall 1985, p. 3.

27. Interview with Cipe Pineles.

28. Joyce Morrow, letter to Barbara Hodik, 13 July 1987.

29. Interview with Joyce Morrow, 17 January 1986.

30. George Hoyingen-Huene, quoted in Seebohm, *The Man Who Was Vogue*, p. 232.

31. M. F. Agha, "Surrealism and the Purple Cow," *Vogue*, 11 November 1936, p. 131.

32. M. F. Agha, "Raphaels Without Hands," *Vogue*, 15 June 1941, p. 144.

33. Agha, "Ralph Steiner," p. 35.

34. George Lois and Bill Pitts, *The Art of Advertising* (New York: Harry N. Abrams, 1977), p. 2.

35. Cipe Pineles, Kurt Weihs, and Robert Strunsky, *The Visual Craft of William Golden* (New York: George Braziller, 1962), p. 23.

Alexey Brodovitch

1. Brodovitch himself gave different years for his birth, from 1898 to 1900. Since errors in birth dates are most often made in favor of youth, 1898 is the more likely. Jerome Snyder gives 1896 as the birth date, but this would mean that Brodovitch was nineteen when enrolled by his parents in the Corps des Pages military academy in 1915. See Jerome Snyder, "51st Annual Exhibition of Advertising, Editorial and Television Art and Design — Inception of the Hall of Fame," *Graphis* 28 (1972–1973), p. 355.

2. Anonymous, "Hospital Interview: Biography of Alexey Brodovitch" (New York, 1963; mimeographed).

3. Owen Edwards, "Zen and the Art of Alexey Brodovitch," *American Photographer*, June 1979, p. 52.

4. Alexey Brodovitch, "Brodovitch on Photography," in *Alexey Brodovitch*, ed. Allen Porter and Georges Tourdjman (Paris: Ministère de la Culture, 1982), p. 123.

5. Alexey Brodovitch Workshop Session, Young and Rubicam Agency, New York, New York, 23 September 1964 (mimeographed transcript).

6. Interview with Sam Antiput, Harry Abrams, Inc., New York, New York, 21 November 1985. Among the problem topics given by Brodovitch during his many years of conducting design workshops were the following: the United Nations, a filling station, national elections, cigarette advertising, renting a car, Penn Station, your neighborhood park, a horse show, hot dogs, a perfume advertisement, a lipstick promotion, a personality, a crumpled piece of paper, a shoe by Dior, the antique show at the Armory, skyscraper tops, Chinese New Year, and Christmas.

7. Allen Hurlburt, *Layout: The Design of the Printed Page* (New York: Watson-Guptill Publications, 1977), p. 31.

8. Edwards, "Zen and the Art of Alexey Brodovitch," p. 53.

9. "Alexey Brodovitch," *Annual of the New York Art Directors Club*, 1972, n.p.

10. Hurlburt, *Layout*, p. 31.

11. "Alexey Brodovitch," *Annual of the New York Art Directors Club*, 1972, n.p.

12. Ben Rose, "A.B.," *Infinity*, June 1971, p. 16.

13. George Herrick, "Alexey Brodovitch," *Art and Industry*, November 1940, p. 169.

14. Alexey Brodovitch, "Critic's Choice," *Popular Photography*, September 1945, p. 31.

15. Brodovitch, "Critic's Choice," p. 31.

16. Charles Reynolds, "Alexey Brodovitch," in *Alexey Brodovitch*, ed. Allen Porter and Georges Tourdjman, p. 120.

17. Interview with Bob Cato, New York, New York, 28 February 1986.

18. Allen Hurlburt, "Alexey Brodovitch: The Revolution in Magazine Design," *Print*, January-February 1969, pp. 58–59.

19. Hurlburt, *Layout*, p. 31.

20. Interview with Sam Antiput.

21. Philip Meggs, *A History of Graphic Design* (New York: Van Nostrand Reinhold, 1983), p. 91.

22. Hurlburt, "Alexey Brodovitch, p. 59.

23. "Alexey Brodovitch," *Annual of the New York Art Directors Club*, 1972, n.p.

24. Charles Reynolds, "Brodovitch," *Popular Photography*, December 1961, p. 92.

25. Jack Anson Finke, "Pro.File: Alexey Brodovitch," *Upper and Lower Case*, March 1975, p. 9.

26. Reynolds, "Brodovitch," p. 80.

27. David Jon Elbin, "A Master Teaches the Experts," *Popular Photography*, January 1955, p. 122.

28. Finke, "Pro.File: Alexey Brodovitch," p. 9.

29. Finke, "Pro.File: Alexey Brodovitch," p. 9.

Charles Coiner

1. Martina Roudabush Norelli, *Art, Design, and the Modern Corporation* (Washington, D.C.: Smithsonian Institution Press, 1985), p. 14.

2. N. W. Ayer was founded in 1869. Among its many pioneering endeavors are a string of firsts: the first to conduct a market survey; to hire a full-time copywriter and a full-time art director; to sponsor a radio program, a network radio program, and a television program; to set copy over two columns; to introduce and emphasize brand names as part of ads and headlines.

3. Norelli, *Art, Design, and the Modern Corporation*, p. 18.

4. Interview with Charles Coiner, Coltsfoot Farm, Mechanicsville, Pennsylvania, 17 January 1986.

5. Charles Coiner Papers, The George Arents Research Library, Syracuse, University, Syracuse, New York.

6. Anna T. Fowler letter, n.d., Charles Coiner Papers, Syracuse University, Syracuse, New York.

7. M. F. Meyer letter, 3 October 1933, Charles Coiner Papers, Syracuse University, Syracuse, New York.

8. Gordon Dean letter, n.d., Charles Coiner Papers, Syracuse University, Syracuse, New York.

9. "Charles Coiner, Art Director," *Portfolio* 2 (1950), n.p.

10. Norelli, *Art, Design, and the Modern Corporation*, p. 19.

11. John Massey, ed., *Container Corporation of America: Great Ideas* (Chicago: Container Corporation of America, 1976), p. ix.

12. Massey, *Great Ideas*, p. ix.

13. Norelli, *Art, Design, and the Modern Corporation*, p. 18.

14. Norelli, *Art, Design, and the Modern Corporation*, p. 19.

15. "Charles Coiner, Art Director," n.p.

16. Interview with Charles Coiner.

17. "Charles Coiner, Art Director," n.p.

18. Charles Coiner, "There Is a Great Need for Tranquility," in "As Artists See Themselves," *The Bucks County Gazette*, n.d., n.p.

19. Charles Coiner, "Out of Tune?" *Art Digest*, 1 February 1936, p. 26.

20. Charles Coiner et al., "What Is the Single Biggest Problem in the Design Field Today?" *Print*, January 1961, p. 53.

21. "Charles Coiner, Art Director," n.p.

22. Neil Harris, *Designs on Demand: Art in the Modern Corporation* (Washington, D.C.: Smithsonian Institution Press, 1985), p. 8.

William Golden

1. Cipe Pineles, Kurt Weihs, and Robert Strunsky, *The Visual Craft of William Golden* (New York: George Braziller, 1962), p. 126.

2. William Golden, "My Eye," *Print*, May 1959, p. 117.

3. Interview with George Lois and Kurt Weihs, at Lois, Pitts, Gershon, and Pon-GGK, New York, New York 28 February 1986.

4. Interview with George Lois and Kurt Weihs.

5. Golden, "My Eye," p. 34.

6. Lou Dorfsman, "William Golden (1911–1959)," *Communication Arts*, Fall 1972, p. 30.

7. Interview with Cipe Pineles, New York, New York, 18 January 1985.

8. Pineles, Weihs, and Strunsky, *The Visual Craft of William Golden*, p. 138.

9. Interview with Cipe Pineles.

10. Pineles, Weihs, and Strunsky, *The Visual Craft of William Golden*, p. 61.

11. Interview with George Lois and Kurt Weihs.

12. Pineles, Weihs, and Strunsky, *The Visual Craft of William Golden*, pp. 139–140.

13. William Golden, "Visual Environment of Advertising," Ninth International Design Conference, Aspen, Colorado, 21–27 June 1959. (The archive of the International Design Conference at Aspen is in the library of the University of Illinois at Chicago.)

14. Pineles, Weihs, and Strunsky, *The Visual Craft of William Golden*, p. 33.

15. Pineles, Weihs, and Strunsky, *The Visual Craft of William Golden*, p. 10.

16. Pineles, Weihs, and Strunsky, *The Visual Craft of William Golden*, p. 126.

17. Pineles, Weihs, and Strunsky, *The Visual Craft of William Golden*, p. 11.

18. Pineles, Weihs, and Strunsky, *The Visual Craft of William Golden*, p. 127.

19. Pineles, Weihs, and Strunsky, *The Visual Craft of William Golden*, p. 142.

20. Gertrude Snyder, "Pro.File: William Golden," *Upper and Lower Case*, December 1975, p. 14.

21. Pineles, Weihs, and Strunsky, *The Visual Craft of William Golden*, p. 13.

22. "William Golden, Hall of Fame," *Annual of the New York Art Directors Club*, New York, 1972.

23. Pineles, Weihs, and Strunsky, *The Visual Craft of William Golden*, p. 127.

Lester Beall

1. Lester Beall and S. S. Field, *DF—A Place in the Country* (1956), p. 4. This promotional brochure, designed and produced by the Lester Beall Design Group, expounded Beall's design philosophy, pictured the Dumbarton Farm (DF) studios, and included a list of Beall's clients.

2. Anna Rothe, ed., *Current Biography* (New York: H. W. Wilson, 1949), s.v. "Beall, Lester."

3. Henry C. Pitz, "L. B.: An Interview with Lester Beall," *American Artist*, March 1949, p. 55.

4. William Golden, "Comments at Typography-U.S.A.," *Print*, January 1964, p. 26.

5. "The New Horizons of Lester Beall," *Interiors*, March 1951, p. 78.

6. "Lester Beall, Inc.," *Industrial Design*, June 1966, p. 104.

7. "Lester Beall, Inc.," p. 104.

8. Lester Beall, "A Plea for the Individual and for Individuality," presentation at the Art Directors Club of New York, 28 March 1964, p. 14.

9. "Lester Beall," *Gebrauchsgraphik–International Advertising Art*, Fall 1939, p. 18.

10. "Obituary for Lester Beall," *The Designer*, October 1969, p. 2.

11. "Obituary," p. 2.

12. Dorothy Beall, "Lester Beall," *Communication Arts*, March-April 1964, p. 7.

13. Lester Beall, "The 'Independent': His Primary Concern Is with Creation," *Print*, November 1958, p. 28.

14. Beall, "The 'Independent,'" pp. 26, 28.

15. Lester Beall, Inc., company self-promotion booklet (Brookfield Center, Conn., 1962), n.p.

16. "Lester Beall, Graphic Designer," *Print*, March 1968, p. 90.

17. "Lester Beall, Graphic Designer," p. 90.

Will Burtin

1. Will Burtin and L. P. Lessing, "Interrelations," *Graphis* 4 (1948), p. 108.

2. Interview with Carol Burtin Fripp and Cipe Pineles Burtin, New York, New York, 25 June 1985.

3. Will Burtin, "International Design Conference," *Print*, July 1955, p. 8.

4. Burtin and Lessing, "Interrelations," p. 109.

5. Ladislav Sutnar, *Visual Design in Action* (New York: Hastings House, 1961), section b/24.

6. George Klauber, "Remembering Will Burtin," *Print*, May 1972, p. 79.

7. Klauber, "Remembering Will Burtin," p. 79.

8. Will Burtin, "The Brain," *Industrial Design*, August 1964, p. 68.

9. Will Burtin, *Visual Aspects of Science* (New York: Upjohn Company, 1964), n.p.

10. "Eastman Kodak Exhibition for the 1964 New York World's Fair," *Industrial Design*, August 1962, n.p.

11. Philip Meggs, *A History of Graphic Design* (New York: Van Nostrand Reinhold, 1983), pp. 376–377.

12. "Obituary: Will Burtin," *Graphis* 27 (1971 1972), p. 514.

13. Quoted in Meggs, *History of Graphic Design*, p. 377.

14. Klauber, "Remembering Will Burtin," p. 79.

15. Klauber, "Remembering Will Burtin," p. 79.

16. Interview with Carol Burtin Fripp, New York, New York, 25 June 1985.

17. Interview with Burton Kramer, Toronto, Canada, 1 November 1985.

18. Klauber, "Remembering Will Burtin," p. 79.

19. Interview with Betti Broadwater Haft, Boston, Massachusetts, 21 September 1985.

20. Interview with Burton Kramer.

21. Will Burtin, "Design and Communication," in *Education of Vision*, ed. Gyorgy Kepes (New York: George Braziller, 1965), p. 78.

22. Will Burtin, "The Means and Ends of Package Designing," *Graphis* 15 (1959), p. 394.

23. Burtin, "The Means and Ends of Package Designing," p. 397.

Alvin Lustig

1. Anonymous, "Alvin Lustig, A Young Man of the West," unpublished manuscript, 1946, p. 2. A mimeographed copy of this manuscript is in the Graphic Design Archive, Rochester Institute of Technology.

2. Ward Ritchie, letter to Elaine Lustig Cohen, 2 November 1982.

3. Philip Johnson, introduction to *The Collected Writings of Alvin Lustig*, ed. Holland K. Melson (New York: Thistle Press, 1958), p. 10.

4. Ritchie, letter to Elaine Lustig Cohen.

5. Alvin Lustig, "Design and the Idea," *Western Advertising*, June 1943, n.p.

6. Alvin Lustig, "Designing, A Process of Teaching," in *The Collected Writings of Alvin Lustig*, p. 13.

7. Lustig, "Designing, A Process of Teaching," p. 25.

8. Lustig, "Designing, A Process of Teaching," p. 13.

9. Alvin Lustig, "What Is a Designer," *Type Talks* 76 (May 1954), p. 6.

10. Danziger recalls that Lustig was teaching at the California Art Center in 1947; however, A. W. Davis in an unpublished 1984 monograph on Lustig indicates that he joined the faculty of the Art Center in 1949. (A. W. Davis, "The Graphic Art of Alvin Lustig," unpublished manuscript, 1984; mimeographed copy in the Graphic Design Archive, Rochester Institute of Technology.)

11. Interview with Lou Danziger, Los Angeles, California, 23 January 1986.

Ladislav Sutnar

1. Ladislav Sutnar, *Visual Design in Action*, with a preface by Mildred Constantine (New York: Hastings House, 1961), C/1.

2. Sutnar, *Visual Design in Action*, 3/c.

3. Joseph V. Bower, letter to Reyner Banham, 16 February 1984.

4. Ladislav Sutnar and Knut Lonberg-Holm, *Catalog Design Progress* (New York: Sweet's Catalog Service, 1950), n.p.

5. Sweet's Catalog Service brochure for *Catalog Design* (New York, 1944).

6. Ladislav Sutnar and Knut Lonberg-Holm, *Catalog Design* (New York: Sweet's Catalog Service, 1944), introduction, n.p.

7. Sutnar and Lonberg-Holm, *Catalog Design Progress*, n.p.

8. Allon T. Schoener, "Sutnar in Retrospect," *Industrial Design*, June 1961, p. 73.

9. "Visual Design in Action," *Print*, September 1961, p. 52.

10. "Visual Design in Action," p. 54.

11. "Visual Design in Action," p. 55.

12. A life member of the New York Art Directors Club, an honorary member of the Czechoslovak Society of the Arts and Sciences in America, and a member of the American Institute of Graphic Arts, Sutnar received, among other awards and recognitions, a silver medal at the Exposition Internationale des Arts Décoratifs Modernes, Paris, 1925; a gold medal at the World Exhibition, Barcelona, 1929; grand prix, Triennale, Milan, 1936; fourteen grands prix and gold medals in various categories at the Exposition Internationale d'Art et Techniques de la Vie Moderne, Paris, 1937; special award of the president, Biennale, Brno, 1968; "Fifty Books of the Year" selection by AIGA in 1950, 1951, 1953, 1954, and 1961; "Fifty Advertisements of the Year," AIGA, 1955; awards in the Product Literature Competition of the American Institute of Architects and Producers Council, 1951, 1952, and 1953; awards in "Design and Printing for Commerce," AIGA, 1949, 1950, 1951, 1952, 1953, 1954, and 1959; exhibitions at the Type Directors Club, 1958, 1959, and 1960; inclusion in "Typomundus 20," a competitive international exhibit of typographic design, 1963; and awards from the Metropolitan Printing Industries, 1962, 1966, and 1967. ["Finding Guide to Ladislav Sutnar Archive 1927–1976" (New York: Cooper-Hewitt Museum, 1985), p. 4. (Mimeographed.)]

11. Hurlburt, "Bradbury Thompson," p. 88. Bradbury Thompson and his wife, Deen Dodge Thompson (m. 1939), have four children: D. Dodge Thompson, chief of exhibition programs for the National Gallery of Art in Washington; Mark B. Thompson, architect and professor at the University of Pennsylvania; Leslie Thompson Keller, a dancer; and Elizabeth Thompson Riley, a painter.

12. Eugene M. Ettenberg, "Bradbury Thompson, Designer in the American Tradition," *American Artist*, April 1955, p. 52.

Bradbury Thompson

1. In an article written in 1952, Georgine Oeri observed that Thompson is a good example of the vital part played by the public libraries in the creative life of the United States, particularly in regions distant from what are considered major centers of culture. [Georgine Oeri, "Inspirations for Printers," *Graphis* 8 (1952), pp. 336ff.]

2. Interview with Bradbury Thompson, Greenwich, Connecticut, 12 December 1986.

3. Gertrude Snyder, "Pro.File: Bradbury Thompson," *Upper and Lower Case* 4 (1977), p. 11.

4. Snyder, "Pro.File," p. 11.

5. "Award-Winning Designer Gives P/A New Look," *Progressive Architecture*, February 1971, p. 27.

6. Snyder, "Pro.File," p. 11.

7. Type Directors Club of New York, *Proceedings of Typography-U.S.A. Forum* (New York: Type Directors Club, 1959), p. 36.

8. Interview with Bradbury Thompson.

9. "Type: Bradbury Thompson 1986," *Print*, November/December 1986, p. 95.

10. Allen Hurlburt, "Bradbury Thompson," *Communication Arts*, January/February 1980, p. 96.

Bibliography

General

Bodine, Sarah, and Dunas, Michael. "Dr. Robert Leslie, 100 Years Old." *AIGA Journal of Grahic Design* 3 (Fall 1985), p. 5.

Gardner, Howard. "Can There Be a Science of Creativity?" Paper presented at the American Society of Adolescent Psychiatry Conference, Philadelphia, 26 September 1986.

Harris, Neil. *Designs on Demand: Art in the Modern Corporation.* Washington, D.C.: Smithsonian Institution, 1985.

Hurlburt, Allen. *Layout: The Design of the Printed Page.* New York: Watson-Guptill Publications, 1977.

Hurlburt, Allen. *The Design Concept.* New York: Watson-Guptill Publications, 1981.

Lois, George, and Pitts, Bill. *The Art of Advertising.* New York: Harry N. Abrams, 1977.

Meggs, Philip. *A History of Graphic Design.* New York: Van Nostrand Reinhold, 1983.

Norelli, Martina Roudabush. *Art, Design, and the Modern Corporation.* Washington, D.C.: Smithsonian Institution, 1985.

Sandusky, B. L. "The Bauhaus Tradition and the New Typography." *PM* 4 (June-July 1938), n.p.

Typo Directors Club of New York. *Proceedings of Typography-U.S.A. Forum.* New York: Type Directors Club, 1959.

Type Directors Club of New York. *Proceedings of Typography-U.S.A. Conference.* New York: Type Directors Club, 1964

University of Rochester. *Proceedings of the Creation Conference.* Rochester, New York, 1987.

Vignelli, Massimo. Interview, in "20th-Century Designers Video Series," Rochester Institute of Technology, Rochester, New York. 1983.

Wild, Lorraine. "Modern American Graphics II: The Birth of a Profession." *Industrial Design,* July-August 1983, pp. 50–58.

M. F. Agha

Agha, M. F. "Leave European Art in Europe." *Advertising Arts,* January 1932, pp. 15ff.

Agha, M. F. "Surrealism and the Purple Cow." *Vogue,* 11 November 1936, pp. 61ff.

Agha, M. F. "Raphaels Without Hands." *Vogue,* 15 June 1941, pp. 19ff.

Agha, M. F. "On Magazines." *AIGA Journal of Graphic Design,* Fall 1985, p. 3.

Agha, M. F. "An Art Director." Agha Papers: The Joyce Morrow Collection. Rochester Institute of Technology, Rochester, New York.

American Printer. March 1935.

Chase, Edna Woolman, and Chase, Ilka. *Always in Vogue.* Garden City, New York: Doubleday, 1954.

"Mehemed Fehmy Agha (Dr. M. F. Agha)." *Annual of the New York Art Directors Club,* 1972.

PM 5: "Agha's American Decade" (August-September 1939). Includes articles by Frank Crowninshield, William Golden, Condé Nast, Arthur Weiser.

Seebohm, Caroline. *The Man Who Was Vogue: The Life and Times of Condé Nast.* New York: Viking Press, 1982.

Snyder, Gertrude. "Pro.File: Dr. M. F. Agha." *Upper and Lower Case* 3 (1976), pp. 4–8.

Alexey Brodovitch

"Alexey Brodovitch." *Annual of the New York Art Directors Club,* 1972.

Alexey Brodovitch. edited by Allen Porter and Georges Tourdjman. Paris: Ministére de la Culture, 1982.

Anonymous. "Hospital Interview: Biography of Alexey Brodovitch." New York, New York, 1963. (Mimeographed.)

Bondi, Inge. "The Photographer's 'Two Masters.'" *Print,* March 1959, pp. 22–29.

Brodovitch, Alexey. "Critic's Choice." *Popular Photography,* September 1945, pp. 31–32.

Brodovitch, Alexey. Workshop Session, 23 September 1964, Young and Rubicam Agency, New York, New York. (Mimeographed.)

Brodovitch, Alexey. Workshop Session, 7 October 1964, Young and Rubicam Agency, New York, New York. (Mimeographed.)

Edwards, Owen. "Zen and the Art of Alexey Brodovitch." *American Photographer,* June 1979, pp. 50–61.

Elbin, David Jon. "A Master Teaches the Experts." *Popular Photography,* January 1955, pp. 48ff.

Ettenberg, Eugene M. "The Remarkable Alexey Brodovitch." *American Artist,* December 1961, pp. 26ff.

Finke, Jack Anson. "Pro.File: Alexey Brodovitch." *Upper and Lower Case* 2 (1975), pp. 8ff.

Herrick, George. "Alexey Brodovitch." *Art and Industry,* November 1940, pp. 164–169.

Hurlburt, Allen. "Alexey Brodovitch: The Revolution in Magazine Design." *Print,* January-February 1969, pp. 55ff.

Konetzka, Michael. "Alexey Brodovitch." Unpublished M.F.A. thesis, Yale University, New Haven, Conn., 1985.

Reynolds, Charles. "Brodovitch." *Popular Photography,* December 1961, pp. 78ff.

Rose, Ben. "A.B." *Infinity,* June 1971, pp. 12ff.

Syracuse University, Syracuse, New York. Arents Research Library. Papers of Charles Coiner: unpublished article on Alexey Brodovitch, June 1963.

Charles Coiner

"Charles Coiner, Art Director." *Portfolio* 2 (1950), n.p.

Coiner, Charles. "Out of Tune?" *The Art Digest,* 1 February 1936, pp. 26–27.

Coiner, Charles. "Guest Editor: Charles Coiner." *Art in Advertising,* 15 November 1954, pp. 6–11.

Coiner, Charles. "The Over-40 AD." *Art Director,* June 1962, pp. 84–85.

Coiner, Charles, et al. "What Is the Single Biggest Problem in the Design Field Today?" *Print,* January 1961, pp. 52–56.

Massey, John, ed. *Container Corporation of America: Great Ideas.* Chicago: Container Corporation of America, 1976.

Syracuse University, Syracuse, New York. The George Arents Research Library. Charles Coiner Papers.

William Golden

Caplan, Ralph. "Cross Section: The Telephone." *Industrial Design,* January 1963, pp. 84–85.

Coffet, Dennie. "William Golden/CBS, The Impact of Corporate Identity." *Print,* January-February 1969, pp. 75ff.

Dorfsman, Lou. "William Golden (1911–1959)." *Communication Arts,* Fall 1972, p. 30.

Golden, William. "My Eye." *Print,* May 1959, pp. 32ff.

Golden, William. "Visual Environment of Advertising." *Proceedings of Ninth International Design Conference,* Aspen, Colorado, June 21–27, 1959.

Golden, William. "Comments at Typography-U.S.A." *Print,* January 1964, pp. 26–28.

Pineles, Cipe; Weihs, Kurt; and Strunsky, Robert. *The Visual Craft of William Golden*. New York: George Braziller, 1962.

Snyder, Gertrude. "Pro.Files: William Golden." *Upper and Lower Case* 4 (1977), pp. 14–16.

"William Golden, Hall of Fame." *Annual of the New York Art Directors Club*. New York, 1972.

Lester Beall

Beall, Dorothy. "Lester Beall." *Communication Arts*, March-April 1964, pp. 44ff.

Beall, Lester. "The 'Independent': His Primary Concern Is with Creation." *Print*, November 1958, pp. 26–29.

Beall, Lester. "A Plea for the Individual and for Individuality." *Proceedings of the Art Directors Club of New York*, Presentation at the Art Directors Club of New York, 28 March 1964, pp. 1–15.

Beall, Lester. "Presentation at Typography-U.S.A." *Proceedings of Typography-U.S.A. Conference*. New York: Type Directors Club, 1964, pp. 10–12.

Beall, Lester, and Field, S. S. *DF—A Place in the Country*. Promotional brochure designed and produced by the Lester Beall Design Group, Dumbarton Farm, Brookfield Center, Conn., in 1956.

"Lester Beall." *Gebrauchsgraphik–International Advertising Art*, Fall 1939, pp. 18ff.

"Lester Beall, Graphic Designer." *Print*, March 1968, p. 90.

"Lester Beall, Inc." *Industrial Design*, June 1966, pp. 102–105.

Lester Beall, Inc. Company self-promotion book. Brookfield Center, Conn., 1962, n.p. Lester Beall Archive, Rochester Institute of Technology, Rochester, New York.

"The New Horizons of Lester Beall." *Interiors*, March 1951, pp. 78ff.

"Obituary for Lester Beall." *The Designer*, October 1969, p. 2.

Pitz, Henry C. "L.B.: An Interview with Lester Beall." *American Artist*, March 1949, pp. 27ff.

Rothe, Anna, ed. *Current Biography*. New York: H. W. Wilson, 1949. S. v. "Beall, Lester."

Will Burtin

Burtin, Will. "Integration: The New Discipline in Design." *Graphis* 5 (1949), p. 230.

Burtin, Will. "International Design Conference." *Print*, July 1955, pp. 8ff.

Burtin, Will. "The Means and Ends of Package Designing." *Graphis* 15 (1959), pp. 392–403.

Burtin, Will. "On Corporate Images." *Graphis* 18 (November 1962), p. 630.

Burtin, Will. "The Brain." *Industrial Design*, August 1964, pp. 66–69.

Burtin, Will. Opening Address, Vision 65. *Vision 65—New Challenges for Human Communications*. ©1966 International Center for the Typographic Arts, pp. 7–10.

Burtin, Will. "Design and Communication." In *Education of Vision*, ed. Gyorgy Kepes. New York: George Braziller, 1965, pp. 78–95.

Burtin, Will. *Visual Aspects of Science*. New York: Upjohn Company, 1964.

Burtin, Will, and Lessing, L. P. "Interrelations." *Graphis* 4 (1948), pp. 108–117.

"Burtin and Upjohn." *Print*, May 1955, p. 36.

"Eastman Kodak Exhibition for the 1964 New York World's Fair." *Industrial Design*, August 1962, pp. 52–55.

"Excerpts from Chairman's Opening Address, International Design Conference in Aspen." *Print*, July 1955, p. 8.

Klauber, George. "Remembering Will Burtin." *Print*, May 1972, p. 79.

"Obituary: Will Burtin." *Graphis* 27 (1971-1972), p. 514.

Snyder, Gertrude. "Pro.Files: Will Burtin." *Upper and Lower Case* 7 (1980), p. 29.

Alvin Lustig

Anonymous. "Alvin Lustig, A Young Man of the West." Unpublished manuscript, 1946. Lustig Archive, Rochester Institute of Technology, Rochester, New York.

Davis, A. W. "The Graphic Art of Alvin Lustig." Unpublished manuscript, 1984. Lustig Archive, Rochester Institute of Technology, Rochester, New York.

Lustig, Alvin. "Design and the Idea." *Western Advertising*, June 1943, n.p.

Lustig, Alvin. "What Is a Designer?" *Type Talks* 76 (May 1954), pp. 2–6.

Lustig, Alvin. *The Collected Writings of Alvin Lustig*, ed. Holland R. Melson, with introduction by Philip Johnson. New York: Thistle Press, 1958.

Ladislav Sutnar

"Finding Guide to Ladislav Sutnar Archive 1927–1976." New York: Cooper-Hewitt Museum, 1985. (Mimeographed.)

Schoener, Allon T. "Sutnar in Retrospect." *Industrial Design*, June 1961, pp. 73ff.

Sutnar, Ladislav. "Commercial Symbols in Architecture." *Architectural Record*, September 1956, pp. 32ff.

Sutnar, Ladislav. *Visual Design in Action*. Preface by Mildred Constantine. New York: Hastings House, 1961.

Sutnar, Ladislav, and Lonberg-Holm, Knut. *Catalog Design—New Patterns in Product Information*. New York: Sweet's Catalog Service, 1944.

Sutnar, Ladislav, and Lonberg-Holm, Knut. *Catalog Design Progress*. New York: Sweet's Catalog Service, 1950.

Bradbury Thompson

"Award-Winning Designer Gives P/A New Look." *Progressive Architecture*, February 1971, p. 27.

"Bradbury Thompson, A Designer's Designer." *Print*, January 1962, pp. 57–60.

Ettenberg, Eugene M. "Bradbury Thompson, Designer in the American Tradition." *American Artist*, April 1955, pp. 52ff.

Grumbach, Doris. "A Handsome, Poetic New Design Is Wrought for the Great Book." *Smithsonian*, June 1979, pp. 73–81.

Hurlburt, Allen. "Bradbury Thompson." *Communication Arts*, January-February 1980, pp. 88–104.

Oeri, Georgine. "Inspirations for Printers." *Graphis* 8 (1952), pp. 336–341.

Snyder, Gertrude. "Pro.File: Bradbury Thompson." *Upper and Lower Case* 4 (1977), pp. 10–12.

"Type: Bradbury Thompson 1986." *Print*, November -December 1986, pp. 95ff.

Type Directors Club of New York. *Proceedings of the Medalist Awards Meeting*. New York: Type Directors Club, 1986.

Index

Numbers in italics indicate
illustrations.